To Dick

Happy Birthday - 1982

Love

Billie

Art in Boxes

Intuition by Joseph Beuys, 1968, wooden box with pencil drawing. Reproduced courtesy VICE Versand and Wolfgang Feelisch, West Germany.

L'Espace d'un Livre (Space of a Book) by Alain Jouffroy, 1966. Reproduced courtesy Claude Givaudan, Paris and Geneva. Photo by François Roussel.

ART in BOXES

Alex Mogelon / Norman Laliberté

VAN NOSTRAND REINHOLD COMPANY
New York Cincinnati Toronto London Melbourne

To The Artists Who Use Boxes For Their Magic

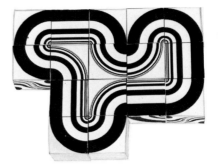

List of Color Illustrations

ALSO BY THE AUTHORS
The Art of Monoprint (1974)
Masks, Face Coverings and Headgear (1973)
Pastel, Charcoal and Chalk Drawing (1973)
   with Beatrice Thompson
Collage, Montage, Assemblage (1972)
Twentieth Century Woodcuts (1971)
The Art of Stencil (1971)
Drawing with Ink (1970)
Drawing with Pencils (1969)
Silhouettes, Shadows, and Cutouts (1968)
Painting with Crayons (1967)

All dimensions indicated are in inches unless otherwise specified.

Van Nostrand Reinhold Company Regional Offices:
New York Cincinnati Chicago Millbrae Dallas

Van Nostrand Reinhold Company International Offices:
London Toronto Melbourne

Copyright © 1974 by Litton Educational Publishing, Inc.
Library of Congress Catalog Card Number 74-5947
ISBN 0-442-24609-9

Art Director: Rosa Delia Vasquez
Type set by V & M Typographical, Inc.

Published by Van Nostrand Reinhold Company
A Division of Litton Educational Publishing, Inc.
450 West 33rd Street, New York, N. Y. 10001

16 15 14 13 12 11 10 9 8 7 6 5 4 3 2 1

The authors and Van Nostrand Reinhold Company have taken all possible care to trace the ownership of every work of art reproduced in this book and to make full acknowledgment for its use. If any errors have accidentally occurred, they will be corrected in subsequent editions, provided notification is sent to the publisher.

Library of Congress Cataloging in Publication Data

Mogelon, Alex.
   Art in boxes.

   1. Boxes in art. 2. Art, Modern—20th century.
I. Laliberté, Norman, joint author. II. Title.
N6490.M585   709'.04   74-5947
ISBN 0-442-24609-9

   1. Boxes in art. 2. Art, Modern-20th century.

CONTENTS

Dark Tower by Lenore Tawney,
1967, wood, ceramics and iron, 12¼
x 4¼ x 4. Reproduced courtesy
Willard Gallery, New York. Photo
by Geoffrey Clements.

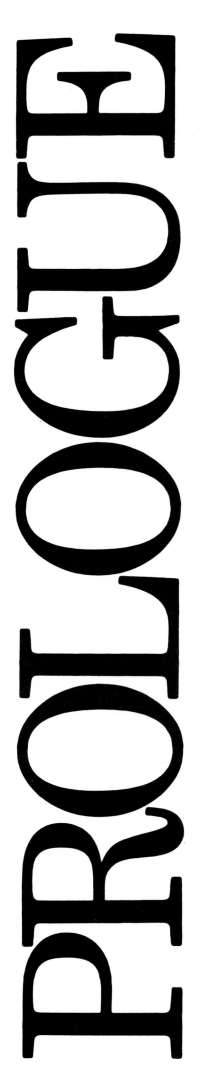

PROLOGUE

No. 1 Kodak camera, 6½ x 3¾ x 3¾. Photo courtesy of Eastman Kodak Company.

Opposite page

Cradle from vicinity of Feucht-wangen, Franconia, Germany, *ca.* 1850. Private collection.
Houses under construction. Photo by William Garnett.
Box car. Photo courtesy Canadian National.
Byzantine sarcophagus, *ca.* 400 A.D.

Boxes have always been an integral part of our life. The incubator, the infant's crib, the baby carriage are all boxes of a sort. Our earliest recollections are of boxes: an empty carton occupied us, the jack-in-the-box amused us, the church collection box mystified us.

When we were children, boxes represented a special kind of magic. Our first snapshot was made by a box which clicked, and pictures which moved were projected by a mysterious box with very special powers. Every big sister had a hope chest stowed away some place in the stillness of the house—a box embracing all that was yet to be. And most boys had a hidden treasure box containing all that had been—gum wrappers, football cards, cigar bands, a half-smoked cigarette, a dead frog awaiting dissection. Many of us saved cookie and cigar boxes for collections of important things like thread and string, buttons, silver foil, china figurines, bottle tops, coupons and foreign stamps.

Who can forget rummaging through trunks and suitcases stored high in the attic or deep in the basement, boxes of "remember when"? And at Christmas time, we contemplated different sized, gaily decorated boxes under the tree, boxes which held the promise of tomorrow.

All good things came and still come in boxes. Apples, appliances, accessories, food, flowers, furnishings, kimonos, kettledrums, kitchen gadgets—most things—are transported across the city or the continent, packed in carton or corrugated boxes, which in turn are stacked in box cars, truck boxes or huge box-like containers to be conveyed in a row or placed in a pile awaiting delivery, purchase, admiration, use, abuse, consumption, abandonment, destruction and oblivion. The box is the conveyor of our needs, our triumphs, our creativity, our ability to produce, our follies, our hang-ups, our memorabilia and finally that which we have reduced to refuse.

The houses and apartment units we live in resemble lookalike boxes, as if we had packed in one large sub-divided carton all we own and all we do, and then shielded it from our neighbors. We call it home. Our entertainment is conveyed by boxes—television sets, stereos, phonographs, radios. We talk to other homes, next door or halfway around the world, through boxes which hold the intricacies of communication. When we travel, it is in steel, stylized boxes of one kind or another, moving on wheels or wings.

The box is part of our everyday language and thinking. We buy boxes of commodities, get theater tickets from a box office, check off boxes in questionnaires, scramble for box seats, fill in crossword-puzzle boxes, watch the baseball box scores and cast our votes in ballot boxes.

Our involvement with and obsession for boxes is incessant and seemingly quite inescapable. From the moment we first open our eyes to the very instant we close them for the last time, the box—as an intriguing and exciting physical form, design or concept—is ever present.

ACKNOWLEDGMENTS

A book of this nature is a cooperative effort, and the authors express appreciation to many individuals and institutions who helped bring it into being.

We extend gratitude to: Alexander Girard of Sante Fe, New Mexico; Jean Brown of Tyringham, Massachusetts; Charles and Ray Eames of Venice, California; Ruth Dyer of the Aldrich Museum, Ridgefield, Connecticut; Dorothy Cameron of Toronto, Ontario; Dianne David, Houston, Texas; Robert Hallock of *Lithopinion*, New York City; Arturo Schwarz, Milan; Carmen Lamanna of Toronto, Ontario; Walter A. Moos, Toronto; Rose Daneswich of *artscanada*, Toronto; Rita Myers and Sharon Mechling of the Museum of Modern Art, New York City; Alfred J. Wyatt of the Philadelphia Museum of Art; Joy Moos of Montreal; Inez Garson of the Hirshhorn Museum and Sculpture Gardens, New York; Claude Givaudan, Paris; Robert Indiana, New York; Maia-Marie Sutnik of the Art Gallery of Ontario, Toronto; Howard Lipman of New York; Linda Traister of New York; Mrs. D. L. Prince, of the Contemporary Arts Museum, Houston, Texas; Count Panza di Biuma, Milan; W. Sutter, Office of Commercial Expansion, Zurich; Lucien Duquette of the Whitney Museum of American Art, New York City.

Our warmest appreciation as well to Sylvia Garber who imaginatively initiated research on the project, to Dorothy Hicks who cheerfully typed and retyped several thousand miles of copy, and to Judith Vanderwall who edited it.

And most of all our sincerest thanks to Marcia Mogelon who was in charge of research and without whom this book would still be some distance from publication.

The West by Robert Baker. Reproduced courtesy of *Lithopinion*, Local One, Amalgamated Lithographers of America, New York.

Robert Baker's great love of history provides the artistic key which fuses boxes and objects together in a meaningful and aesthetic unity in his *Collages in Boxes* series. "I've always thought that it must have been great to live in the time of the steam railroads and riverboats," Baker says: "At the time of the Civil War and the earlier West, too. Those values—openness and adventuresomeness—still hold up, and I hate to see them lost."

He refers to his boxes as "a blend of nostalgia and authentic romance . . ." in which he is recreating both history and the very spirit of an era. Historical validity, relevance, texture, size relationships, depth and dramatic impact are the vital ingredients to the success of his compositions, boxes which vividly bring to life something of the excitement and spirit of the days when America was young.

Vega 4 Cercles (positif) by Victor Vasarely, anodized metal, 17 x 17 x 17 cm. Reproduced courtesy Éditions Denise René, Paris.

Vasarely has mastered optical exploration of planar surfaces; his compositions are structural in accordance with precise mathematical formulae and are both rhythmical and symmetrical, while his color is highly disciplined and serves to emphasize aspects of form. Many times, Vasarely's patterns or geometrical compositions seem to pulsate or generate movement as precise ascending, descending or multiple units and regimented color assault the eye. This illusion of motion is induced by a number of disciplines which Vasarely has mastered, including rigid geometric patterning, juxtapositioning of precise black geometric forms, use of shapes or designs with white or open space as well as the varying of size and arrangement of colors, circles, squares and shadings to produce bulging or bubbling effects (see page 38 for the negative of this composition). Through his use of contemporary materials, plastic and metallic surfaces, Vasarely has become one of the foremost innovators in exploring interaction between form and color.

Box constructions by Wolfgang Walther. Reproduced courtesy of the artist.

The artist achieves overall effects by fixing colored designs on paper behind the ball and box, which are transparent and can be made to appear vastly different in structure or extremely alike through treatment with color. Color has the ability to create the appearance of form within form, illusions, marbleized or crystallized effects, or the feeling of opulence. The transparent quality of the forms acts somewhat like a microscope in which the viewer can see enlarged or isolated sections of the color design.

The artist, Wolfgang Walther of West Germany, is primarily concerned with the effect of his color on the viewer. "... I want to unfold a 'story' on the surface which is constantly being viewed," he says. "I try to ... call on the unknown viewer for a response ... details and at times the colors are the tools of success ... intuition, particularly fantasy, is important ..."

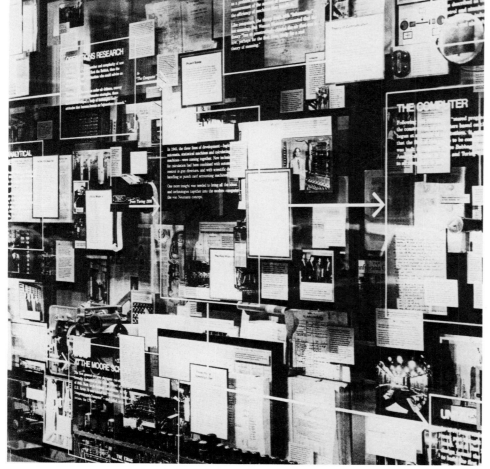

Above. A partial view of a large box display case from A Computer Perspective, an exhibition on the origin and development of the computer that was conceived and assembled for International Business Machines Corporation by the Office of Charles and Ray Eames. *Left.* A detail from the display which, with its myriad compartments and inserts, is probably the most complex box ever created. Reproduced courtesy of International Business Machines Corporation, Office of Charles and Ray Eames, Howard University Press, publisher of *A Computer Perspective.*

The exhibition consisted of six tall glassed boxes, each eight feet high, which constituted a "history wall", tracing the many origins and social patterns which led to the evolution of modern computer science from 1890 to 1949. The exhibition, through a multiplicity of three-dimensional grids displaying photographs, documents, and actual instruments, produced a strong kinetic quality; objects seemed to appear and disappear depending on the viewer's location and point of concentration. This exhibition technique, coupled with a series of color-coding systems, enabled the viewer to trace the development of computer sciences as if he or she were living at each time and in each environment which hastened the process of development.

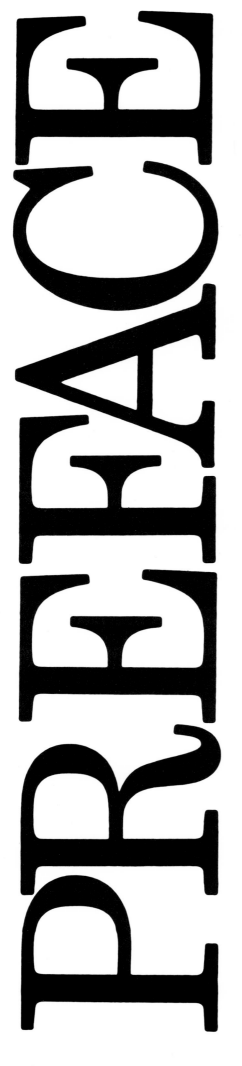

PREFACE

Allegory of the Missionary Work of the Jesuits by Padre Andrea Pozzo, 1691–1694, fresco ceiling of the nave of S. Ignazio, Rome.

In this excellent example of *trompe l'oeil,* the artist fully succeeds in "deceiving the eye" through a complex scheme of drawn and painted architecture, in which the perspective produces an illusion of recession, diminishment or depth. The success of many *trompe l'oeil* compositions is dependent on the position of the viewer, for frequently movement from a precise location renders the painting ineffective. Pozzo's example is an exception. Illusionistic paintings such as this and *Design for a Stage Set* (top, opposite page) employ techniques in composition, perspective and foreshortening, not only to convey three-dimensional, box-like effects on a flat surface, but moreover to give the impression that the composition telescopes itself into infinity.

Opposite page

Above. Design for a Stage Set by Giuseppe Galli Bilbiena, engraving by J. A. Pfeffel, 1740.

Center. Jack-in-the-box from the early 19th century. Reproduced courtesy of The New York Historical Society, New York City. A spring, concealed in the loose burlap around the figure, is nailed to the bottom of the box and is activated when the lid is opened.

Below. The reclining figure of the Pharaoh Tutankhamen in its wooden coffin, Egyptian, 14th century B.C. Reproduced courtesy Griffith Institute, Ashmolean Museum, Oxford.

The figure bears a dedication, "to external life," from Maya, who was an attendant of the pharaoh's necropolis. The inscription is one of the few expressions of personal attachment found in the king's tomb.

Art in Boxes was born several years ago when in the course of research and of simply looking, we became aware of an increasing number of artists both in North America and abroad, working in what we called (perhaps for the want of a more explicit or technical term) "boxes".

The genre we were looking at (if it can qualify as a genre) was interdimensional, perched at some almost indiscernible and, yes, indescribable point between working on the traditional flat surface and what we commonly know as sculpture. It soon became apparent that rarely did two of our box artists work in the same manner, nor were too many of them aware of the fact that they were doing something unusual or different. We began to see various styles and schools of box making—the nostalgia or memory box, the stop action, where-did-the-person-sitting-at-this-table-go-to? box in the technique of Spoerri, the pell-mell multiple avalanche of boxed objects and things created by Arman, the archetypal imagery of Tony Urquhart, the celestial box fantasies of John Willenbecher, the humorous Roy Fridge conceptions, the iconographic constructions of Vin Giuliani. There was soon a most formidable list.

Everything has a beginning of some sort and in time, a point of historic emergence. Was this a movement and if it was, what could we say of its origin? Feeling a little like a baseball team in a park which incomprehensibly lacked a diamond or bases to touch, we looked to the past for some sort of historic emergence. At the same time, we contacted hundreds of artists working in boxes to attempt to ascertain why this format appealed to them and to learn more of their individual techniques. In this latter respect, our inquiries soon became part of a chain reaction. We would discover an artist working in boxes and he or she would soon enthusiastically tell us of a friend working in a similar vein who, when he or she was contacted, would put us in contact with still another artist working within this frame of reference. The unusual thing about this is that each of these artists, for the most part, seemed to work in an entirely different environment, with vastly different materials and in completely different directions. As the examples depicted in this book indicate, it was a landslide of artists working in a manner, shape and form yet to be acknowledged and perhaps still to be clearly defined and categorized.

The decorative box can be found in one form or another throughout human history. The ancient Egyptians buried their pharaohs in caskets bedecked and adorned with images and hieroglyphics pointing to the journey of the departed royalty into the next world. The history of the synagogue, the church, the mosque and the temple is rife with boxes and cabinets revered and highly decorated in the form of altars or reliquaries in which sacred scrolls and holy objects are enshrined. The early primitives made boxes principally for carrying and storage, and, despite the hardships of day-by-day living, adorned these with carvings, painted

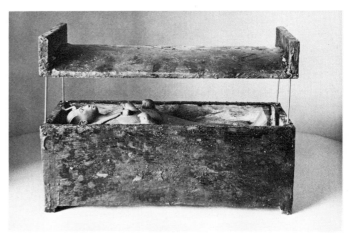

15

designs in symbols and images and objects such as shells, bones, feathers and quills. It appears that boxes and people have always been inseparable.

A box, as contrasted with a square or rectangle, implies the illusion of depth or three real dimensions. One of the earliest formal examples of attempting to achieve another dimension with but the basic two is the hinged diptych, which goes back to the Greek and Roman eras. In the Middle Ages, the diptych became popular as a two-paneled altarpiece, its surfaces usually consisting of carved or painted biblical or historical events. Soon triptychs, hinged three-paneled pieces for the most part depicting religious scenes, became popular in churches and continued to be prevalent up to the 17th century. In the 5th century the Greek artist Zeuxis is said to have painted a cluster of grapes with such dimensional realism that birds flew through his window in an attempt to peck at them. That was perhaps the first recorded version of *trompe l'oeil*. During that era in art history known as

Left. The coffin lid of Thent-Muten-kebti, Egyptian. *Right*. The coffin lid of a priestess, Egyptian. Reproduced courtesy British Museum, London.

The highly decorated interiors of the coffins of Amenemapt and Nes-Mut, Egyptian. Reproduced courtesy British Museum, London.

Italian Baroque and Rococo (15th century) paintings which gave the box-like appearance of depth became highly popular throughout Europe. Employing the technique of composition and perspective, illusionistic painting on a two-dimensional plane conveying the feeling of three-dimensional space was quite common and practiced by a number of individual painters in Italy, France, Germany and Holland for several centuries, though it never had the status of an artistic movement.

In the 19th century, three-dimensional graphic designs—many achieved through ingenious folding of materials—were prevalent in the box-like presentation of the European greeting-card and paper-novelty business. For the most part, these were romantic, frilly and a far cry from fine art.

The still-life painting of William Michael Harnett (1848–1892) is perhaps a forerunner to the emergence of the box environment as we have tried to represent it. Working on a flat surface, Harnett meticulously painted objects, almost in collage formation, which had predominant three-dimensional *trompe l'oeil* qualities to them. Frequently he would paint a frame around his composition, giving the impression that his objects were somehow resting in a box. The collage painting of John Haberle in the late 1800's also has this built-in appearance of dimensionality.

This same artistic solution—the idea of framing or boxing a composition, particularly a collage—can be seen in the early work of Picasso (1881–1973). His famous *Still Life With Chair Caning* has a length of rope circling and framing it, as if to prevent the various painted and pasted elements from falling out of the composition. Kurt Schwitters (1887–1948) executed a number of similar pieces, each held together by a box or frame, in his so-called "exaltation of mundane" collages and assemblages. Similarly, a glimmer of box-like tendencies can be discerned from time to time in the work of some artists in the Cubist, Dada and Surrealistic movements through a variety of techniques involving the enclosing and revealing of open space.

If the work of one artist must be isolated as the embryo of *Art in Boxes*, it is perhaps that of Marcel Duchamp (1887–1968). In 1913, Duchamp's first "ready-made," or manufactured, objects emerged. They were coffee cups, bicycle wheels, shovels, things seen and used by almost everyone on an everyday basis, exhibited as non-sculpture. In time they succeeded in challenging the traditional concepts of art. By selecting an item, removing it from its traditional surroundings and placing it in a totally new environment, Duchamp was eminently successful in giving his object great impact through being seen entirely in a new context. His *Fountain*, a 1917 ready-made that consisted of an ordinary urinal, is a celebrated example. A founder of the American Dadaist movement, Duchamp and his ready-mades, many of them boxes of some shape or form, have in their own way stimulated and inspired artists to explore the box phenomena in directions that are personal, highly individual and most unique.

The box artist of today has been further stimulated by found objects, the discards of our "disposable" society, as well as by the new materials of the 20th century—urethane, aluminum, plastic foam, epoxy, neon bulbs, plastic, nylon, polystyrene, incandescent bulbs, vinyl, Plexiglas, cellulose—the list expands with each technological development.

None of this mini-history succeeds in establishing the box environment as either a genre or a movement. Being neither art critics nor historians, it is far from our intention to try to do so. We want *Art in Boxes* to bring attention and prominence to what we think is still another new tendency within contemporary art, journeying somewhere between painting and sculpture and many times hanging mysteriously between illusion and reality.

ALEX MOGELON/NORMAN LALIBERTÉ
Montreal/New York
April 2, 1974

Below. Pennsylvania Chest (Berks County type), *ca*. 1780, yellow pine and poplar, 28⅝ x 52½ x 23. Reproduced courtesy The Metropolitan Museum of Art, New York, Rogers Fund, 1923.

Above. Religious statue of San Francisco de Assis, New Mexico, 1800–1850, cottonwood, in original niche. Collection Marion Koogler McNay Art Institute, San Antonio, bequest of Marion Koogler McNay. Reproduced with kind permission.

Right. Statue of Nuestra Señora del Carmel (Virgin of the Scapular), New Mexico, 19th century, cottonwood, in original niche. Collection Marion Koogler McNay Art Institute, San Antonio, bequest of Marion Koogler McNay. Reproduced with kind permission.

Above. Valise by Marcel Duchamp, 1943, leather case containing reproductions of the artist's work, 16⅛ x 14¾ x 4⅛. Collection, The Museum of Modern Art, New York, James Thrall Soby Fund. Reproduced with kind permission.

Below. Boite-en-Valise (Box in a Valise) by Marcel Duchamp, 1941–42. Reproduced courtesy Philadelphia Museum of Art, Louise and Walter Arensberg Collection. Photo by A. J. Wyatt.

Duchamp is the originator of the "Ready-mades," man-produced, almost everyday objects which, with little change or alteration, become works of art. Here two leather-covered boxes produced in multiple copies have been sectioned into a series of fold-out compartments containing miniature reproductions of Duchamp's paintings and three-dimensional objects. They are virtually portable museums in themselves.

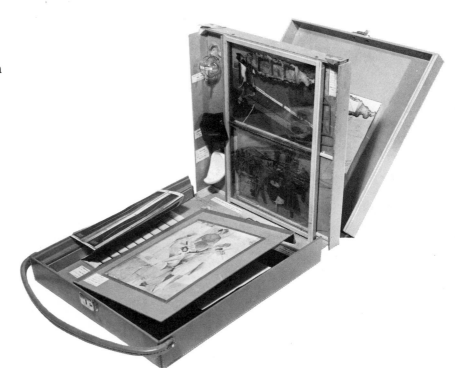

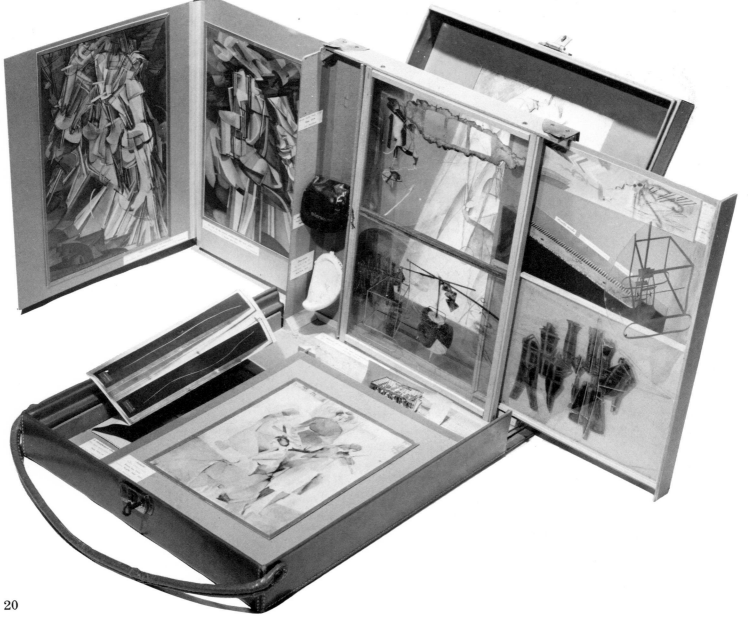

Left. Nose by Alberto Giacometti, 1947, bronze, 31⅞ high. Reproduced courtesy Hirshhorn Museum and Sculpture Garden, Smithsonian Institution, Washington, D.C.

Below. Bruit Secret (Hidden Noise), Ready-made, ball of twine by Marcel Duchamp, 1916. Reproduced courtesy Philadelphia Museum of Art, Louise and Walter Arensberg Collection. Photo by A. J. Wyatt.

Below. The Captured Hand by Alberto Giacometti, 1932, wood and metal. Reproduced courtesy Kunsthaus, Zurich, bequest. Photo by Walter Dräyer.

All three of these boxes are open and yet at the same time project the feeling of inescapable captivity. Giacometti's cage-like boxes are surrealistic in quality; he reduces the human figure or parts of it to an almost skeletal minimum to suggest the insecure and transient condition of mankind.

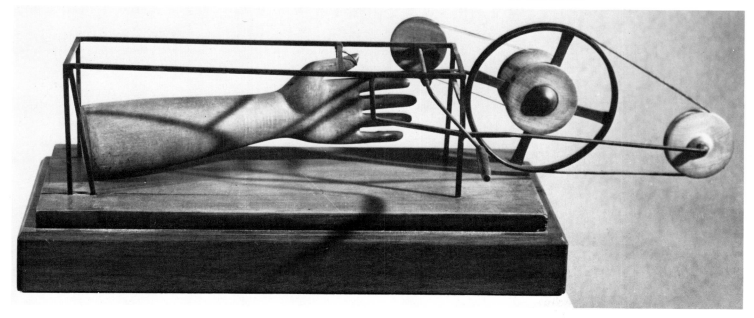

Two Children Threatened by a Nightingale (2 enfants sont menaces par un rossignol) by Max Ernst, 1924, oil on wood with wood construction, 27½ x 22½ x 4½. Collection, The Museum of Modern Art, New York, purchase. Reproduced with kind permission.

The effect of Ernst's box construction is heightened by the appearance and placement of other box shapes within the composition that illuminate the story and convey a feeling of mystery and of almost unending depth. The gate, the post and the wall of the building are made of wood, and accentuate the foreboding quality of the work.

Toy kitchen, American woodwork of the late 18th century. Reproduced courtesy The Metropolitan Museum of Art, New York, the Sylmaris Collection, gift of George Coe Graves, 1930.

This toy kitchen is a box with one side open. The miniature stove, cabinets, shelving and tiled flooring produce a box-within-a-box effect.

Perspective box of a Dutch interior by Samuel von Hoogstraten (1627–1678). Reproduced courtesy The Detroit Institute of Arts.

A student of Rembrandt, von Hoogstraten is best known for his architectural and perspective fantasies. Are the sides of this box-like composition produced by mirrors or is the mirror effect produced by an articulate artist?

Object by Joan Miro, 1931, painted wood, steel, string, bone, bead, 15¾ x 8¼ x 4¾. Collection The Museum of Modern Art, New York, gift of Mr. and Mrs. Harold X. Weinstein. Photo by Eric Pollitzer. Reproduced with kind permission.

Cage by Alberto Giacometti. Reproduced courtesy Nationalmuseum, Stockholm. Miro's object is rough hewn, a series of nailed-together planks, a dowel-like turret and a large spike piercing an unknown entity. Giacometti's *Cage* possesses a series of objects, which though finely shaped are nevertheless unrecognizable. Both compositions suggest feelings of endless captivity and perhaps even eventual execution.

24

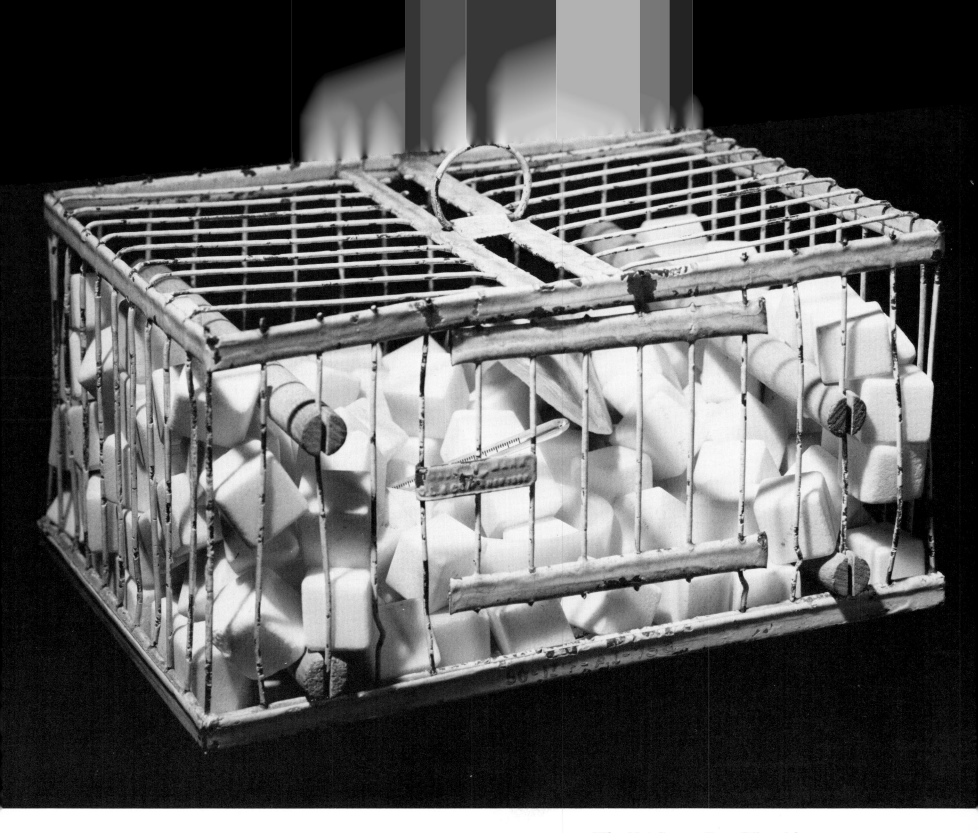

Why Not Sneeze Rose Sélavy? by
Marcel Duchamp, 1921, Ready-made
of marble blocks in the shape of
lump sugar, thermometer wood and
cuttlebone in a small bird cage, 4½
x 8⅝ x 6⅜. Reproduced courtesy
Philadelphia Museum of Art, Louise
and Walter Arensberg Collection.
Photo by A. J. Wyatt.

Duchamp's definition of art embodies
the axiom that all objects made by
man are in themselves works of art.
A pioneer of the Dada movement,
Duchamp frequently attached the
name "Rose Sélavy" to his compositions that included found objects.

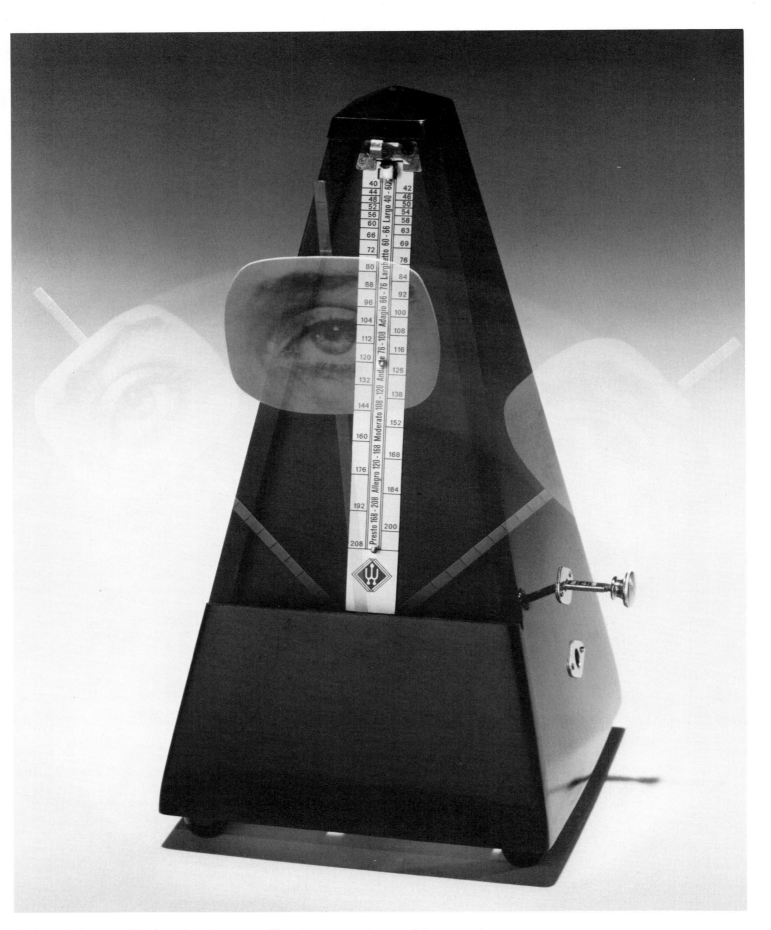

Object Indestructible by Man Ray, 1958, a cut out photograph of an eye has been affixed to the metronome. Reproduced courtesy Philadelphia Museum of Art, Louise and Walter Arensberg Collection. Photo by A. J. Wyatt.

Man Ray experimented in a number of media including airbrush, photography and film. Much of his work is in the humorous vein and yet at the same time projects elements of mystery. In motion, the humor of the metronomic eye soon surrenders to a feeling of hypnotic mystery.

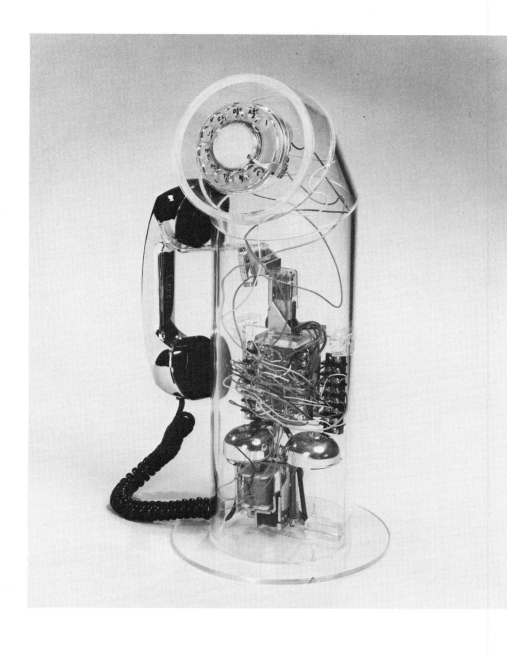

The periscope telephone designed by Bruce Wasserman. The inner mechanism of a working telephone encased in an unusually shaped see-through box makes an exciting composition. Reproduced courtesy TeleConcepts Inc., Hartford, Conn.

Pages 28 and 29

Habitat '67, Montreal, Moshe Safdie, architect. Reproduced courtesy of the architect.

The show-piece of Expo '67, Habitat projected a unique architectural concept—a series of box-like apartments piled on each other so as to create a pyramidal shape of geometrically stacked boxes. In this revolutionary idea the roof of one unit (or box) provided the open-air terrace or landscaped garden for the living unit (or box) above it.

Habitat suggests a new concept of urban living, providing the convenience of the downtown apartment with the spacious privacy of the suburbs. Every window corner offers an exciting view, for no unit overlooks the other. The complex is 12 stories high and was originally composed of 158 one-to-four bedroom apartments built of prefabricated concrete boxes weighing some 85 tons each and hoisted into place by a mammoth crane device. These boxes support each other much like children's blocks piled in a helter-skelter pyramid-like form. The complex includes a skywalk, children's play areas and miniature parks, while each living unit has its own patio and garden. Habitat was expanded following Expo '67; it is fully occupied, and apartment space within it is in great demand.

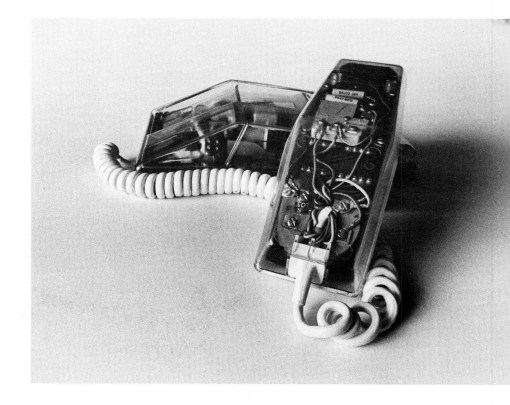

Plexiglas encased Contempra phone. Reproduced courtesy Bell Canada. Photo by Alan Bowering. Colored wires combine with multi-colored transistorized elements to form an abstract box composition.

Description of Table by Richard Artschwager, 1964, formica, 26¼ x 32 x 32. Collection of Whitney Museum of American Art, New York, gift of the Howard and Jean Lipman Foundation, Inc. Photo by Geoffrey Clements. Reproduced with kind permission.

The painting of the box form gives the illusion of a table. Through color, design and texture the tablecloth, legs and dimensions of the table have been cleverly delineated.

Cube 6 + 3 by Jiro Takamatsu, wood and lacquer, 15 x 15 x 15 cm. Reproduced courtesy Tokyo Gallery, Tokyo.

From the simple cube to pull and draw boxes and on to Westermann

Unlike the artist's preparation for painting on canvas or drawing on paper, his first concern with respect to the box he has constructed or chosen to work with is how to cope with the additional dimension of depth and how to approach the limitations of area and space to which he has confined the eventual composition.

In a sense, the box shape, which is a simple cube or dimensional variations of a cube, is pure art within itself. The stark simplicity and beauty of *Intuition* by Joseph Beuys (see page 1) is a good example of this. For the artist, the challenge is to make the viewer forget or bypass the basic shape, and he uses that shape as a stepping-stone towards communicating the concept of something else entirely. Richard Artschwager's *Description of Table* (opposite page) is a case in point, where clever conceptional design transforms the block form into another entity.

This chapter demonstrates how a number of artists have achieved nearly infinite variations on boxes through their application of different approaches and techniques. Some have used the extremely simple linear element to obliterate the original box shape, transforming it into another entity. Others have hidden the three-dimensional qualities of the box by creating numerous divisions and segments within it. Victor Vasarely (see pages 38 and 10) employs *trompe l'oeil* devices to give depth and the effects of movement to the sides of his cube. Still others have kept their boxes intact but by adding hinges have been able to extend the cube (and aspects of its space) in other directions.

The cubic space within the box presents many challenges. Many artists have explored this challenge by setting a box within another existing space, which may or may not be cubic. When such an environment is completely foreign to the viewer, it frequently will create disturbing emotions. *Forest Door* by Ian Carr-Harris (see page 41), for instance, evokes a surrealistic, almost mythological sense of fatality.

Throughout this chapter there are many examples of the imaginative work of H. C. Westermann. By his unique placement of architectural, human and mechanized forms, Westermann projects imagery that is surrealistic and at the same time highly contemporary. In all instances, whether they are Westermann's paradoxical compositions or the highly inspired and very individual work of Roy Fridge or Varujan Boghosian, the artist succeeds admirably in transforming the original box concept or format to an entirely new entity, an entity which communicates with subtlety or dynamism despite the artistic limitations imposed by the hard planes and angles of the box format. Frequently it is by accepting the challenge of these self-imposed limitations that the artist produces his most creative work.

Untitled by Robert Morris, 1966, reinforced fiberglass and polyester resin, 36 x 48 x 90. Collection of Whitney Museum of American Art, New York, gift of the Howard and Jean Lipman Foundation, Inc. Photo by Geoffrey Clements. Reproduced with kind permission.

Robert Morris believes that boxes can do varied and contradictory things. "The box form," he says "can reveal, hide, enclose, expose, hang, stand free, be held, clarify, mystify, surprise and be easily portable or sendable. I try to use these advantages to the maximum, even to the point of collaborating with the box on the initial idea since boxes literally emanate usages and histories.

"I try to use materials as the logical extension of ideas and since the physical probabilities within the enclosing capabilities of a box are extensive, I find myself using complex technical means. In one box I've used wood burning tools, acrylic paint, silverpoint drawing, photographs, modeling paste, glass and found objects. The problem then becomes making these diverse elements work together."

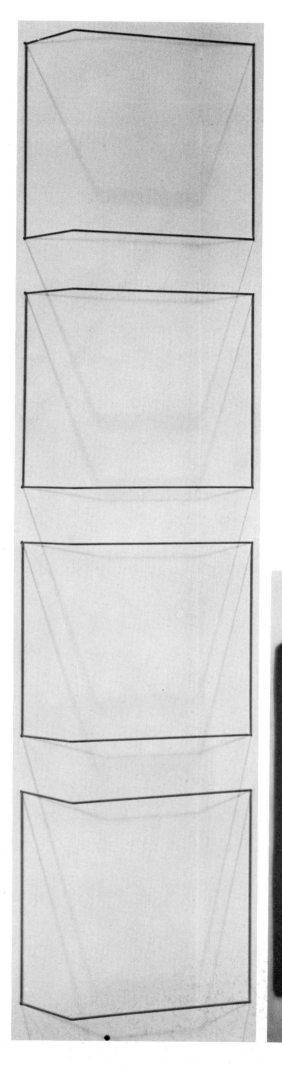

Left. Four Unit Untitled by Fred Sandback, 1968, elastic cord, steel rod, pointed fluorescent blue paint, 69 x 14 x 7. Collection of Whitney Museum of American Art, New York. Photo by Geoffrey Clements. Reproduced with kind permission.

Center. No. 11 Wall Plaque by Chryssa, 1960, plaster on wood. Reproduced courtesy Locksley/Shea Gallery, Minneapolis.

Right. Work No. 18, 1938, New York by Charles Biederman, painted wood with clear and yellow plastic. Reproduced courtesy of the artist.

Three different artists working in different materials take the box concept in three different directions. Sandback uses cord, paint and steel rods to define box areas and to suggest other enclosures, which are ghost-like and may or may not exist. Chryssa's box is definite; it has the texture of concrete but may well be Styrofoam (plastic foam). The box by Biederman has eight sides and suggests a number of different inside levels; because of our pre-conceived notion of what a box should look like, we cannot comprehend it fully with but an initial glance.

Pages 34 and 35

Relief R 69–34 by Jan Schoonhoven, hardboard, carton, and paper, 104 x 104 cm. Photo courtesy Stedelijk Museum Amsterdam.

Kwadraten Relief by Jan Schoonhoven. Reproduced courtesy Museum Amsterdam.

Schoonhaven's work appears to be an endless procession of boxes within boxes. The repetition of pattern creates illusions of depth, which in turn spawn innumerable sequences of light and shadow that tend to distort and vary shape, relief and density. The repetition also produces qualities of motion and movement as seen in the earlier example by Vasarely. Although these boxes are made of white cardboard, which we know as a flat substance, there is a great sculptural or relief quality to them which is created by the depth of scoring and the amount of light allowed to penetrate each individual indentation.

Below. Study for Orpheus by Varujan Boghosian, 1963, wood and metal, 12 x 12 x 6½. Reproduced courtesy of the artist. Photo by John D. Schiff.

This simple box, composed of but two basic objects, has a great dramatic impact. The box itself appears to have survived a century of wear and tear, while the sphere or globe (despite or perhaps because of the fact that it is boxed) seems to be suspended in an almost endless expanse of space. The nails in the sphere suggest people and/or continents. It all comes together in a spirit of mystery and wonderment.

Left. Prisoner by Walter Yarwood, 1962, found object and welded steel, 22½ high. Reproduced courtesy Art Gallery of Ontario, Toronto.

The tightly wound, barbed-wire effect succeeds in closing out both space and light, and in creating what must be a formidable prison. Still, the viewer remains aware that this prison is being seen from the outside looking in.

Below. A Flux Atlas by Bob Watts, stones from Bob Watts Farm, Martins Creek, Pennsylvania; Basement, Wooster St., New York; Stonington Beach, Maine; Island's End, Green Port, Long Island; Garbage Dump, Naxus Island, Cyclades; Provoacao Beach, San Miguel Island, Azores. Produced by Fluxus. Reproduced courtesy Archive Jean Brown, The Shaker Seed House, Tyringham, Mass.

This is a very personal study in geography for the artist; stones and objects gathered from the different sites and places he has visited come together in a plastic box to form his own visual atlas.

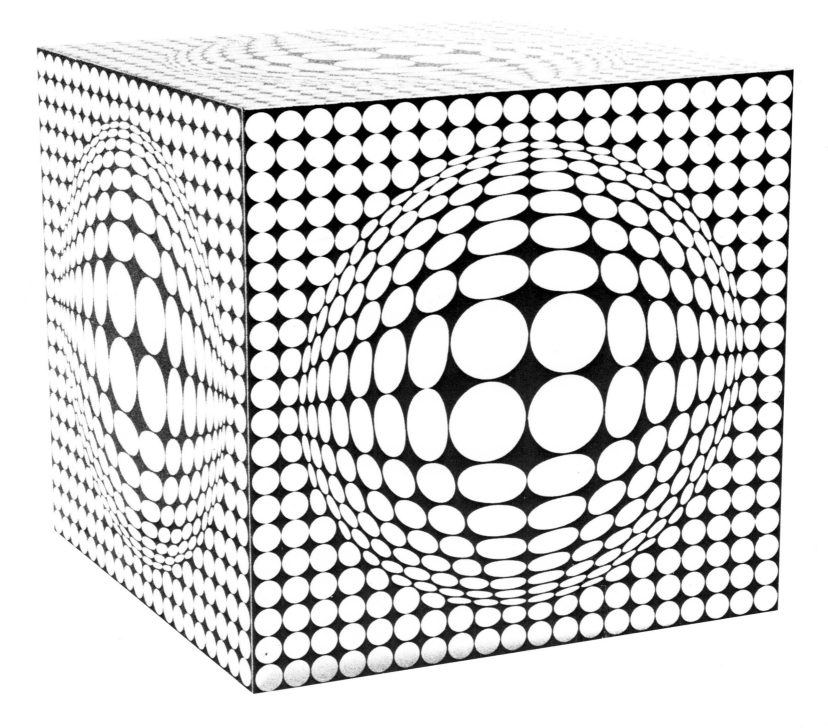

Vega 4 Cercles (negatif) by Victor
Vasarely, anodized metal, 17 x 17 x
17 cm. Reproduced courtesy Éditions
Denise René, Paris.

Variations of the size of the circles
or dots in sharp geometrical perspective—coupled with the manipulation
of coloring—succeed in giving the
frontal view of this box both a feeling of movement and a bulging,
extra-dimensional effect. Note how
the front design, when used on the
left surface or side of the cube,
appears flat and far less dimensional, and contrast this negative
pattern with the positive shown on
pages 10 and 11.

April Strolling by Alexander Calder, 1965, Japanese clay, 19¾ x 19¾ x 19¾. Collection of Whitney Museum of American Art, New York, gift of the Howard and Jean Lipman Foundation, Inc. Photo by Geoffrey Clements. Reproduced with kind permission.

Best known for his mobiles and stabiles, Calder has created a fascinating and playful box. The split at its center suggests that it comes apart, but what does it contain? Is the inside the reverse of the outside? It has that dramatic feeling about it, perhaps achieved by the random placement of spheres or by their absence.

Box That Never Closes by Michael Craig-Martin, 1967, blockboard, white polyurethane, glass, 24 x 24 x 24. Reproduced courtesy Rowan Gallery, London.

At first, the unusual shape of the over-all box (or is it a cluster or grouping of boxes?) strikes the viewer. The next thought is to differentiate between what is the inside and what part is the outside of the box. Title and tilt combine, producing a desire to close the form visually.

4 identical boxes with lids reversed by Michael Craig-Martin, 1969, blockboard with chrome hinges, 18 x 18 x 24. Reproduced courtesy Rowan Gallery, London.

Center. The viewer seeing the back of the boxes notes that they are hinged and therefore capable of opening. This produces curiosity about the inside of each of them.

Below. The boxes have been opened and turned to face the viewer, who has the distinct impression that they contain twice the space or area than when seen from the previous position.

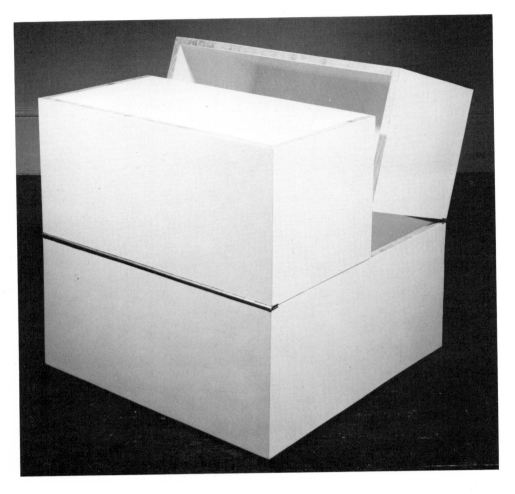

3 Stoppages Etalon (3 Standard Threads) by Marcel Duchamp, 1913–14, three threads glued upon three glass panels (each 49⅜ x 7¼) and three flat wooden strips, separating the curve of the threads (averaging 45 inches in length), wooden box (11⅛ x 50 x 9). Collection The Museum of Modern Art, New York, Katherine S. Dreier Bequest. Reproduced with kind permission. The intricate division of space and the unique materials Duchamp has used combine to give this box a lyrical presence. It is no longer a simple collection of objects, no longer even an art object—it is pure visual poetry.

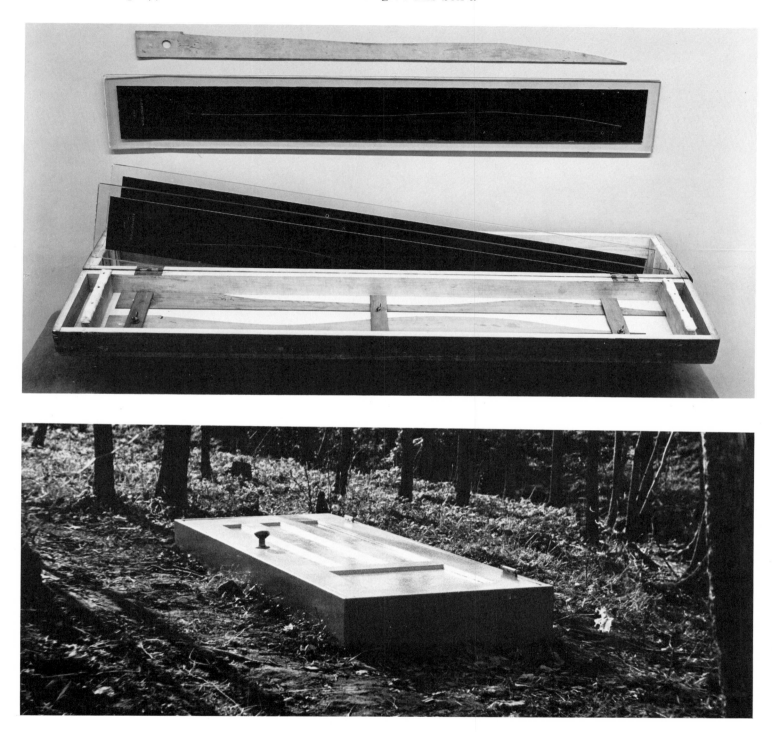

Forest Door by Ian Carr-Harris, 1968, wood, 8 x 28 x 78. Reproduced courtesy Carmen Lamanna Gallery, Toronto.

You don't expect to see a door in any position but upright; to add to the surprise, you don't expect to see a door on the forest floor. What is behind it? Is the box a tomb, does it represent a legend or is it all some sort of macabre joke or statement? There is something ominous about it . . . perhaps it's best to leave curiosity unsatisfied.

Ian Carr-Harris likes details. "Details," he says, "detract their origins so you can really see a lot of stuff often not intended or significant. I like insignificant things because they offer room for manoeuvre and definition outside the limits of their original content.

"Materials as such are of no decisive importance to me. I use logical and simple construction materials or equipment sufficient to present my thoughts in as uncomplicated a manner as possible, and requiring as little 'material' awareness as possible consistent with normal perception."

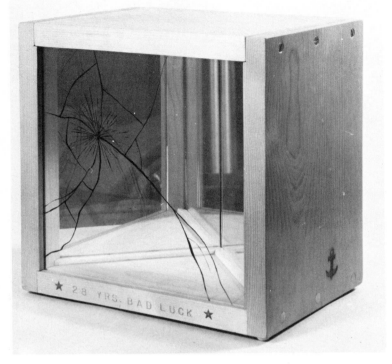

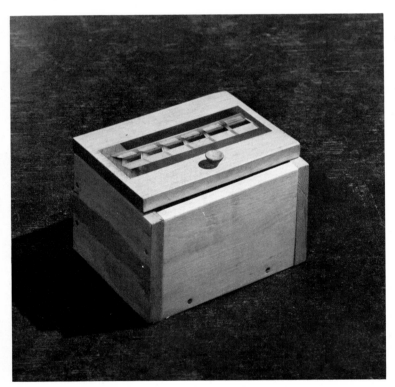

Top left.

Untitled by Donald Judd, 1971, stainless steel, 54 x 96 x 144. Reproduced courtesy Leo Castelli, New York.

Donald Judd's surfaces evoke a somewhat sensuous feeling. Though he is a Minimalist, each of his constructions and boxes states its very own presence clearly and emphatically, and the feeling of expansiveness and freedom projected is far in excess of the space actually occupied.

Top right.

28 Years Bad Luck by H. C. Westermann, 1964. Reproduced courtesy Museum of Art, Rhode Island School of Design, Providence; from the Small Works from the Richard Brown Baker Collection Exhibition, 1973.

The broken front glass on this box (either painted on or actually broken) combined with the clever placement of mirrors inside the box itself contribute to the viewer's illusion of seeing four different broken mirrors.

Bottom, left and right.

Box Piece (open and closed) by Reinhard Reitzenstein, 1972, wood, photographs and ashes, 6½ x 10 x 8. Reproduced courtesy Carmen Lamanna Gallery, Toronto.

A box for a fantasy field trip has six different compartments for the collection of specimens. A photo affixed to the closed lid shows an open box, while the one on the inside of the lid shows the same box closed.

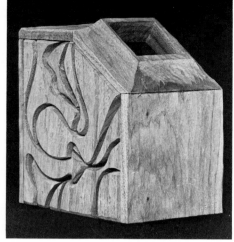

Left Column

Above. Surface Boxes by Richard Prince, 1972, wood and plaster, 5½ x 5½ x 3½ each. *Below left. Spring Landscape.* Collection of K. Prince. *Below, right. Winter Landscape.* Collection of Equinox Gallery, Vancouver. Both by Richard Prince, 1971, wood, plastic, polyurethane foam and paint, 3 x 4½ x 3. Reproduced courtesy of the artist.

A box is a box until it is opened; then it becomes what is inside of it. Richard Prince's box compositions come in many different forms—wooden containers, former pickle jars, drawers, parts of soda-pop crates. There is a sense of landscape and season about much of his work that transcends the initial impressions of playfulness. The viewer becomes involved with and committed to participation in the ideas Prince projects, even though some of his boxes have a disarmingly small physical presence.

Right Column

Boxes by Roy Fridge. *Top. Pierce Arrow—Hasty Heart Cinema Box. Center. The Dear Heart—Clear Heart Redwood Box. Bottom. The Little Red Heart Part Box, The Spiky Ball Box,* and *The Lower Borer Box.* Reproduced courtesy The David Gallery, Houston.

In the box at the top, the principal attraction is what cannot be seen. What will a look into the aperture reveal? Though there are many attractions to the box at the center, the viewer is fascinated by the handle. What will pop out by turning it? (See page 68 if you are very curious.) The boxes in the photo at the bottom represent an irresistible challenge when closed. One simply must open the door so that all may be revealed.

43

i really, DON'T know, WHAT to say
(closed and open) by Aleksander
Danko. Reproduced courtesy of the
artist. Photo by Douglas Thompson.

The exterior of the box, covered
with bold but soft Japanese-like
brush strokes, resembles a painting
on canvas. A harsh metal plaque
has been affixed to the lid, indicating
that the interior may be mechani-
cally complex. The inside is somewhat surprising for it turns out to
be almost the antithesis of the outside; its plaque, cushioned on felt
layers, reads: "I really don't know
what to say." Has the viewer been
fooled or is there a deeper hidden
meaning?

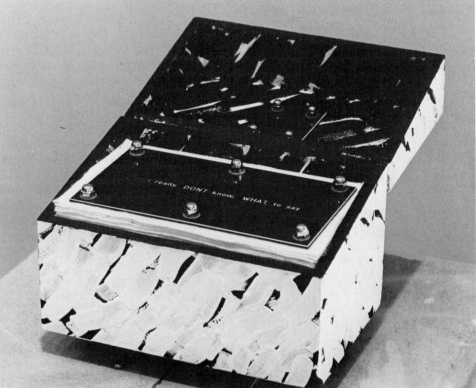

Opposite page

An Old Indian Implement by H. C.
Westermann, 1971, Connecticut field-
stone, Douglas fir, walnut and pigskin, 16½ x 10 x 10¾. Reproduced
courtesy Allan Frumkin Gallery,
New York. Photo by O. E. Nelson.

The implement is an ordinary well-
rounded field rock, but the almost
monumental housing which Westermann has given it—a well-made,
precision-hinged walnut case lined
with padded pigskin—brings out the
somewhat humorous or satirical
implications of the title as well as a
deeper contrast between the initial
simplicity and later sophistication
of man's use of materials.

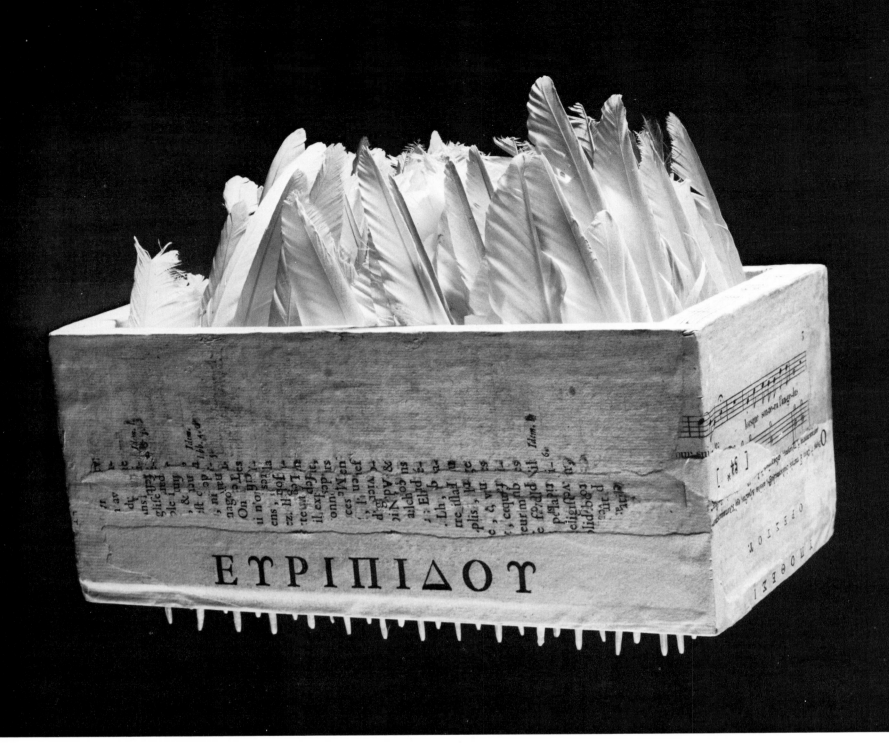

Album of White Music by Lenore
Tawney, pigeon feathers, wood,
paper, 9¾ x 5½ x 4½. Reproduced
courtesy the Museum of Contemporary Crafts, New York, from the
exhibition Furs and Feathers, 1971.
Photo by Ferdinand Boesch.

This white on white, almost nest-like
box with its musical notes and words
projects a rhythmic, almost lyrical
feeling all its own. The juxtaposition
of different alphabets and the textured qualities of the box itself
produce an effective graphic under-
tone while the entire composition
evokes a mood of poetic serenity.
The principal Greek word on the
side of the box reads "of Euripides."

Ponte Vecchio by K. H. Hödicke, 1972. Reproduced courtesy Galerie René Block, Berlin. Photo by Hilde Zenker, Berlin.

In this extremely clever, super-graphic idea the artist not only conveys a semblance of Ponte Vecchio but also a dynamic over-all view of an entire city through the use of a bent aerial photograph and two old bricks. The bricks portray something of the history and antiquity of the city depicted in the photograph.

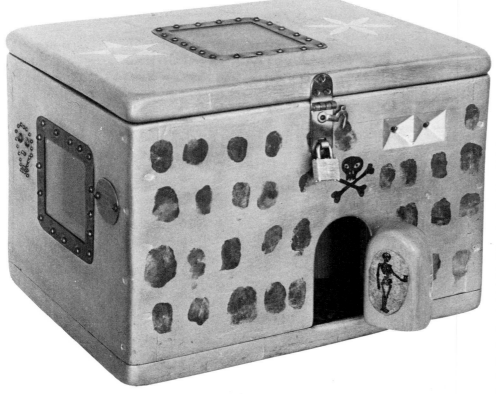

Box by H. C. Westermann, 1957, pinewood, dovetail construction, oil base and shellac finish, 8½ x 12 x 9¼. Reproduced courtesy of Betty Asher. Photo by Alfred Lutjean.

Westermann's box is whimsical and projects a naive sense of humor. It's padlock, the thick doll-house-like door, the curious pieces of hardware nailed to the top and side, the dabs of paint and the skull and crossbones all contrive to suggest a chapter from *Robinson Crusoe,* a scene out of the *Pirates of Penzance* or a box in which a child would hide all his worldly treasures.

The Dancing Teacher by H. C. Westermann, 1972, copper, lead, glass and wood, 21 x 28 x 17¾. Reproduced courtesy of Allan Frumkin Gallery, New York. Photo by O. E. Nelson.

The screening material used gives the glass-encased house an over-all feeling of transparency while the welded materials serve to create the illusion of a staircase and other objects. The doors, windows and human figure seem to float. Even the chimney and dormer on the roof of the house have a ghostly x-ray quality to them. Note the cat climbing at the inside left of the glass case outside the house.

Westermann combines found objects with those which he manufactures himself, and places them in juxtaposition within boxes to create constructions that range from the literal to the surrealistic and satrical. The simplicity of his approach to subject matter and the almost pure and perfect quality of his wooden constructions serve to create a great impact on the viewer. Is *An Old Indian Implement* (see page 45) really an ordinary field rock or is there a deeper meaning to it, something that is being smoke-screened by the sheer simplicity confronting the audience?

Westermann succeeds admirably in disturbing the viewer's natural expectations by placing together in a composition materials and objects which are opposites to each other. His imagery is disarming though often humorous, for what at first seems to be an enlargement on the ridiculous evokes deeper feelings on closer examination and introspection.

Yellow House and Death Ship by H. C. Westermann, 1972, walnut, vermillion and pine, 15 x 8⅜ x 15⅞. Reproduced courtesy Allan Frumkin Gallery, New York. Photo by O. E. Nelson.

The Log Cabin by H. C. Westermann, 1968, maple, beech, pine, redwood, walnut, leather, glass and enamel, 19 x 19 x 14½. Reproduced courtesy Allan Frumkin Gallery, New York. Photo by Nathan Rabin.

Though the forms or shapes of these two houses (and the one on the previous pages) are similar, the variations within each are limitless.

Yellow House and Death Ship is opaque; everything happening is on the outside. The house is highly polished, the grain and texture of the wood, the simple drawings representing the window and door, as well as the face on the end of the house are intentionally left bare. In *The Log Cabin*, everything is completely open. The door, window, shingles and chimney are rendered with much attention to detail, and the viewer has the distinct impression that this is a happy home. Yet, despite its openness, one does not see any more of its inside than of the inside of *Yellow House and Death Ship*, which projects an ominous feeling about its hidden contents.

The World by Varujan Boghosian, 1965, wood and ceramic blocks, 24 x 14 x 10½. Reproduced courtesy of the artist. Photo by Stephen K. Scher.

"The materials I used in my first constructions were limited to children's blocks, small old boxes, croquet balls and a few odds and ends. Since then I have taken advantage of ironing boards, tools, ball-bearings, barn doors, numerous dolls, children's toys, scientific instruments, bones, rags, and an endless assortment of textures and geometric forms. When I collect, it can be for a specific construction in progress or because from past experience I feel intuitively that the forms under consideration have the qualities that may work well in relationship with other pieces."

In this box by Boghosian, the stack of tiny mosaic-like blocks fits together almost perfectly to form what appears to be a strong, orderly pile. Still, the suspended ball menaces it. Will the block arrangement withstand the fall of the weapon, or will it capitulate, like the beautiful, well-built brownstone structures of another era, to the wrecking-ball of so-called progress?

Page 52

The Rainbow by Varujan Boghosian, 1971, wood, glass and steel, 36 x 30 x 8. Reproduced courtesy Cordier & Ekstrom, Inc., New York. Photo by Dartmouth College Photographic Service.

The fan-like rainbow gives the effect of a crown, the wire grid cleverly uses a halo effect to achieve a sense of holiness and sanctity, while the triangle and the three circles symbolize the trinity in this box that suggests the religious imagery of an icon.

Little Egypt by H. C. Westermann, 1969, fir and pine, 68 x 31 x 31. Reproduced courtesy of Allan Frumkin Gallery, New York. Photo by Eric Pollitzer.

A full-sized, highly polished wooden door and casing with a platform leading to it inevitably produces a sense of exploration. The use of materials differs from Ian Carr-Harris' *Forest Door* (see page 41) and yet the incongruity of the placement of elements yields the same sense of intrigue.

Sit on the Floor by Bob Kinmont, 1971, Douglas fir and sage, 23½ x 23½ x 7. Reproduced courtesy of the artist. Photo by Jack Fulton.

This box was made for an exhibition in a large hall in the San Francisco Museum. The artist built a 9 x 12 foot room within the hall, with its own door, and placed his box on its floor. In order to see the contents of the box the viewer had to enter the private room and sit on the floor, obeying the words engraved on the lid, and open the box. For the curious, this was a public situation transformed into a very private viewing.

The Gingerbread Cabinet by Spring Hurlbut, 1971, gingerbread, brown conté pencils, felt-tipped pen and brown colored pencil, 25½ x 40½ x 3½. Reproduced courtesy *artscanada*, Toronto. Photo by Eberhard Otto.

The understatement of detail makes the viewer conscious of the two main elements in this box, one three dimensional, the other flat. The physical box represents an oven, the flat shadow-like painting of the figure blossoms into a real baked gingerbread man.

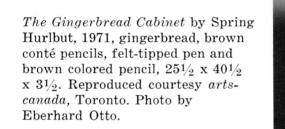

Cake Box with Six Finger Paintings & Favours, full view and detail, by Mary Janitch, 1973, 15 x 10 x 10. Reproduced courtesy Carmen Lamanna Gallery, Toronto.

A discarded pastry box and shells placed at random within it, are the principal elements of this composition which projects a buried-treasure feeling with a rusted watch suggesting the great amount of time required for an oyster to develop its own treasure. Mary Janitch believes in "total involvement" with a piece in its "happening." She lives with objects before they are assembled, and they become "a part of my everyday living . . . a part of me as they grow . . ."

Webster and Cigars by Larry Rivers, mixed media, collage on wood construction, 13¼ x 16 x 13¼. Reproduced courtesy Marlborough Gallery, Inc., New York. Photo by O. E. Nelson.

The lid of the box has been elegantly painted, which is somewhat of a parody on the box's supposed function of holding cigars. Perhaps an aristocratic importance is being suggested for the men who will smoke the cigars. The cigars themselves are dowels with painted bands for labels. Though the mock functionalism is retained throughout, there is no doubt that the box is a work of art in the most complete sense.

Oyster, cigar, dream and secret boxes

Through art, the artist can become a magician, a mystic, a prophet, creating compositions which walk the tightrope between the real and imaginary, compositions which evoke a response primarily because of their ambiguity. As surrealist, he uses totally familiar objects in ways that remove them from the everyday world, which awaken old images in the viewer, from his past or the depths of his psyche, to deal with the incongruity. Each of us creates a new work of art from the same piece because we have different personalities, shaped by individual human experience and values.

Familiarity serves to disarm our ordinary set of perceptions, and leaves us free to experience the artist's unusual treatment of materials. Cigar boxes, tables, desks, drawers, filing cabinets are not merely isolated, forcing us to see new artistic values in them as Marcel Duchamp's Ready-mades did, but are manipulated or recreated to confront us with a brand-new set of symbols.

These are not simple cubes, although they may be sparsely dealt with. Instead of challenging the box composition's rigid structure of lines, planes, angles, and space, the artist of the dream box focuses on what the box contains (even if that is precisely nothing) and what it serves as protection against. Each of these compositions holds as many secrets and fantasies as we can find in our own psyches.

Opposite page

A Jomo Collaboration—McMana-way/Camblin by David McManaway, 1971. Collection Pete and Lesley Schlumberger, Houston. Photo by Hickey and Roberston. Reproduced with kind permission.

David McManaway "finds things" and makes constant use of them. "I seem to have an eye that is forever finding things. My source is simply going out through the front door. I've been accused of employing a front runner who deposits things in my path (the street, stores, some-one's house, etc.) I bring the things I find into the studio and hang them on the wall or stand them on shelves —these objects fill my studio with visual ideas—they become objects with extended meanings over and above their obvious intent . . . My studio has been called a 'memory bank'; I like this definition because I believe the creative process is an employment of memory in a very specialized way . . ."

Double-Nose/Purse/Punching Bag/Ashtray by Claes Oldenburg, 1968–1970, vat-dyed cowhide, suede one side; redwood; cast bronze; reversible zipper, non-separating; leather-covered bible paper book; stamped wooden discs; redwood chips. Reproduced courtesy of the artist and Gemini Gel, Los Angeles. Photo by Malcolm Lubliner.

The ashtray and nose images were cast in bronze by the lost wax process from the original clay models created by the artist, while the leather bag was hand-crafted from his original muslin mock-up. The carpentry on the redwood box, as well as the woodburning of the nose-lock image, were also made from the original Oldenburg mock-ups. The wooden walnut discs, produced in 1¾-inch and ⅞-inch diameters, were hand rubber-stamped, and the original drawing by the artist which appears on the inside lid of the box was silkscreened. The paper book is covered in deerskin leather with the title blind stamped; text pages were hand set and hand printed by letterpress on bible paper (synthetic parchment).

Oldenburg has rejected the concept that sculpture must be hard in substance and permanent in appearance. His soft sculptures, made of many materials such as leather, vinyl, canvas, cotton and plastic sheeting, project aspects of the materialism of 20th-century life. In them, he completely rejects the traditional concept of sculpture as form created by carving away a surface or material or, conversely, building it up. His objects, conceived on a grand scale, often have much humor, animation and human appeal. Through them, Oldenburg seeks to enlarge both the boundaries of artistic expression as well as the viewer's concept of everyday life.

Above, left. Finger Box Set (No. 21) by Ay-O, 1968, mixed media, 12 x 17¾ x 3¾. Reproduced courtesy of Milwaukee Art Center. Photo by P. Richard Eells.

Above, right. Weekend, a suitcase containing the announcement for an exhibition of the works of Beuys, Brehmer, Hödicke, Hutchison Köpcke, Polke and Vostell. Courtesy of Edition René Block, Berlin. Reproduced with kind permission. Photo by Hilde Zenker.

Below. Filing System, The Danko 1971 Aesthetic Withdrawal Kit (closed and open) by Aleksander Danko. Reproduced courtesy of the artist. Photo by Douglas Thompson.

The *Finger Box Set* presents the viewer with a briefcase containing fifteen individual boxes, each with an aperture, appearing to be very much alike. Each box, however, evokes a different emotion, for all are completely dissimilar inside. The content of one is rough, another smooth, still another slippery and so forth.

Weekend has a foreign-intrigue quality, with its various compartments and built-in dividers. The viewer begins to feel like the person who did the packing—he has a compulsion not to miss a thing.

The *Aesthetic Withdrawal Kit* is nothing more than a regular steel drawer file for 3 x 5 index cards, and yet here, too, curiosity gets the better of the viewer because of the intriguing title. When you pull the drawer open, disappointment is but momentary, for the artist—through his simple message sitting in the index-card slot—shifts the onus onto the viewer. Suddenly you are responsible for a reaction to what you see! The box contains nothing but one's own reaction to the artist's words, which is all his outside label promised you in the first place, and which prompts the feeling that some boxes are best left unopened.

Left. Monster Package Deal No. 1, closed and open (detail) by Aleksander Danko. Reproduced courtesy of the artist. Photo by Douglas Thompson.

Below, left. Dr. West Outfit Container by Bob Kinmont, Douglas fir, men's clothing, 24 x 24 x 31. Reproduced courtesy of the artist.

Below, right. Just for the Record by Ian Carr-Harris, 1972, painted pine, 42 x 30 x 18. Reproduced courtesy of Carmen Lamanna Gallery, Toronto.

Monster Package Deal No. 1 is more complicated in appearance than Danko's *Filing System* on the previous page, but the effect is somewhat the same. The sign on the lid, combined with the way the box has been constructed, tends to sharpen the viewer's sense of anticipation. The inside of the box is a contradiction: one does not expect to see the traditional shape for love—the heart— engraved with anything but a sentimental message. The heart sits in a padded depression much like a casket, while the soft painting on the inside of the lid seems to be in direct opposition to the hard, metallic-like substance used to make the heart.

Dr. West Outfit Container is an old-fashioned school desk holding the clothing worn by a Dr. West, whose presence and performance in the San Francisco area was considered to be somewhat eccentric. The artist believes that Dr. West was "a pure person, capable of listening. His performance seemed to be his way of sharing." Sadly, the clothing, in its museum-like case, strongly suggests that this type of personality is a part of the past.

Just for the Record has a nostalgic, distant feeling about it. On first view, one can only surmise what's in it, although it looks like an old school desk or a case in which a doctor once kept surgical instruments. The box can be easily opened, but one cannot be sure whether it is safe to examine the contents.

Above, left and right. Names (full view and detail) by Ian Carr-Harris, 1972, varnished wood, 55½ x 29 x 29. Reproduced courtesy of Carmen Lamanna Gallery, Toronto.

Below, left and right. Nancy Higginson 1949 by Ian Carr-Harris, 1971, painted wood, 53½ x 16½ x 18. Reproduced courtesy of Carmen Lamanna Gallery, Toronto.

Illusions of space, loneliness and abandonment are projected by the artist through these boxes, which seem to have been left behind, perhaps because they contain memories of days long past.

Above. Railroads (left) and *River-boats* (right) by Robert Baker. Reproduced courtesy *Lithopinion*, Local One, Amalgamated Lithographers of America, New York.

Robert Baker's boxes are pure nostalgia, visual reminiscences of a colorful and romantic era in America's history. His vision of *The West* is shown on page 9.

Center column and right column, top. A selection of boxes by Bill Tunberg. Reproduced courtesy of the artist.

Bill Tunberg uses a multitude of different materials in his box constructions including, glass, wood and rope. These boxes have a locked-in look or quality about them, their contents appearing to be doomed to eternal imprisonment.

Right column, center and bottom. The Swiss Pavilion at Expo '70, Osaka, Japan. Reproduced courtesy Trade Fairs and Special Events Office, Suisse d'expansion commerciale, Zurich.

Further details on the box constructions of the Pavilion of Switzerland appear on page 200.

Right. Coney Island by Sandra Jackman. Reproduced courtesy of the artist.

Sandra Jackman believes that art is a form of direct communication. "The materials I use have to hold a mystery for me, individually first, and then in combination—like an ink-blot test. I am putting together environments from memory and/or impressions. These all are very personal and have great meaning to me."

Below. The Circus by Sandra Jackman. Reproduced courtesy of the artist.

Left. Kroa A by Victor Vasarely, 1970, polychrome anodized metal, 50 x 50 x 50 cm. Reproduced courtesy Editions Denise René, Paris.

Right. Cloud Box by Sas Colby, 1973, silk box with satin clouds, beads and photo transfer appliqué, 5 x 5 x 5. Reproduced courtesy of the artist.

Sas Colby's soft upholstered boxes are inventive, full of charm and playful. Her day box (exterior) is warm with a bursting sun and floating puffy clouds, while the night box (interior) is blue, tranquil and serene.

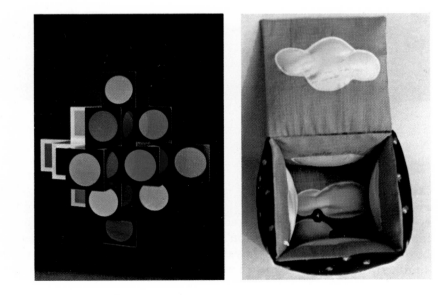

Autobiographical Box by Sas Colby, 1973, silk with appliqué photo transfers and glass window in back, 5 x 5 x 8. Reproduced courtesy of the artist.

The people boxes

We live, work, travel, play, and suffer in box-like environments, and the depiction of a figure in a box is often easily recognizable as a person in a room, a prison, a shop—anywhere the artist chooses to identify or to leave enticingly vague. If the box is large, real people can be used as part of the art object, with profoundly evocative results. Whether imaginary or real, the human form involved in a box situation calls forth an emotional participation from the viewer that requires a completely different set of values and standards than the usual aesthetic response.

It requires a great sensitivity on the part of the artist too, because people are much more vulnerable objects than apples, for instance, or dream images. Whereas the slicing of an apple is an unemotional viewing experience, harm—actual or implied—to the human figure evokes deep feelings of fear and repulsion. The closed shape of a box implies limitation; therefore setting a figure in a box frequently suggests imprisonment. *Mana Idol* and *Oedipus as a Young Boy* (see page 67) are sensitive renderings of a human situation much more disturbing than the imprisonment of a mere object.

In creating people boxes, the artist must become concerned with the implied treatment of people-as-objects, because the situation radiates a sense of reality that makes it much harder for the viewer to remain conscious that these, after all, are merely symbols.

Memorial to the Idea of Man by H. C. Westermann, wood and brass, 55 x 24. Collection of Mr. and Mrs. Louis Manilow, New York. Photo by Nathan Rabin. Reproduced with kind permission.

There are many elements of human culture projected by this Westermann box. At first one sees aspects of a castle, a grandfather clock or a game at Coney Island, but then a religious connotation seems to take form, shaped by the stance of the Buddha-like arms, with an open mouth suggesting prophetic words and a single eye reminiscent of Greek mythology. One has the feeling that the box may well contain a torah, or sacred scroll.

Mana Idol by Ivan Eyre, 25 x 11 x 15. Reproduced courtesy the Winnipeg Art Gallery, gift of MacLaren Advertising Co. Ltd. Photo by Ernest Mayer.

Ivan Eyre's *Mana Idol* appears to stand in a void, a prisoner unto himself. Though there are no bars or doors in front of him, the figure is uncomfortable and strange, appearing to be in bondage to his own thoughts and complexes.

Oedipus As A Young Boy by Sidney Simon, 1961, laminated walnut, 34 inches high. Collection of Arthur T. Hadley, Jr. Photo by Thomas Feist. Reproduced with kind permission.

This work represents a period of panic for Sidney Simon. It was created when the cold-war period was at its height, and some were preparing underground shelters against the threat of atomic warfare. The boy standing in his box looks to the heavens; whether it is in a spirit of hope or with a feeling of terror is a matter of conjecture.

Top and center. Dear Heart—Clear Heart Redwood Box, unoccupied and occupied, by Roy Fridge. Reproduced courtesy The David Gallery, Houston.

Bottom. An exhibit of boxes by Roy Fridge at The David Gallery, Houston. The pyramid-topped box is called *The Multi-Tiered, Many-Triggered, Whirling War Arrow.* Reproduced courtesy The David Gallery, Houston.

Instead of placing a sculpted figure into a box, Roy Fridge has built his *Redwood Box* to contain an actual human being. By sitting in the box, the viewer becomes much more than a viewer. The box has moving parts, can be open or closed (see page 43), and parts of the human body can be isolated by being projected through the holes and cutouts in the box. All of this serves to distort a viewer's sense of human physiology and anatomy when a human figure occupies the box (to say nothing of the perceptual distortion experienced by the enclosed person).

Opposite page

The Butcher Shop by George Segal, 1965, plastic, wood, metal, vinyl and Plexiglas, 94 x 99¼ x 48. Reproduced courtesy Art Gallery of Ontario, Toronto, gift of the Women's Committee Fund, 1966.

George Segal described his first sculpture (*Man at the Table,* 1961) as a ". . . Duchampian-Dadaist gesture—a ready-made person at a ready-made table." Segal's "life-casting" techniques depend, as he says ". . . on the sitter's human spirit to achieve total effectiveness." He studies gestures, positioning and postures, then section by section encases individuals in plaster. After uniting the section he reworks the exterior surfaces to achieve the desired result, then places the assembled figures in a life-like everyday setting.

Segal considers *The Butcher Shop* a prime example of an environment composed in terms of planar design, pointing to the dimensional effect created by the various elements within the box-like ship. He contrasts this with the highly sculptured form of the butcher's human body, a form which is in contradiction to its movie set kind of environment. To the viewer, the *Butcher Shop* is still another example of man being boxed in, both physically and spiritually, by his means of earning a livelihood.

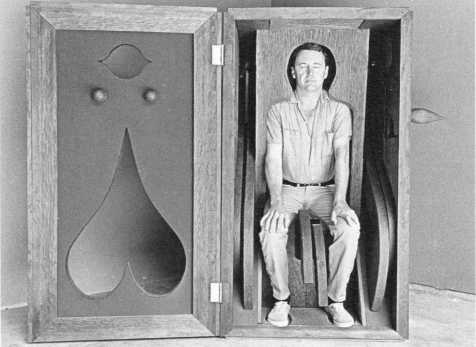

Above. An open doorway, a table in which a TV and an open briefcase rests, a mirror, a bed on which a nude girl sits, a bald-headed man sitting on a chair, a nude girl, an empty chair, a potted plant (two details) by Gerald Crimmins, mixed media. Reproduced courtesy Henri Gallery, Washington, D.C.

The boxes by Crimmins assume a life-size, stage-like scale while the use of mirrors creates the illusion of more figures being present than actually are there.

Right. My Own Castle (two views) by Gordon Wagner, 1972, a kinetic box. Reproduced courtesy of the artist.

"Objects can be banal and cute, I try to reject them. It is easy to fall into a trap of banality. So my selectivity must be high. I use many dissimilar objects in a more surreal juxtaposition to form some sort of poetic statement. The object by itself is not enough. Any object that lives by itself should never be introduced to another subject. Therefore I like broken or incomplete objects so they may transmit with another object to make a new image . . ."

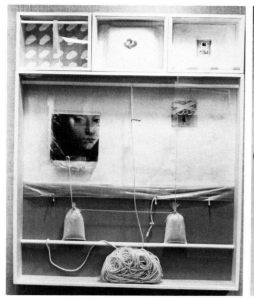

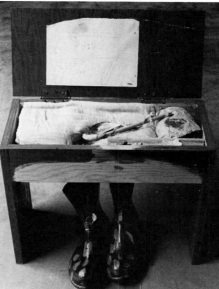

La dame, la corde, et les deux sacs (The woman, the string, and the two sacks) by Irene Whittome, 1973, assemblage, 48 x 61 x 5½. Reproduced courtesy Galerie Martal, Monreal.

Irene Whittome has divided her box into different compartments, each containing symbolic imagery through the use of odd objects. The composition is united with string or twine, and yet each section tends to pull against the other.

Bench With My Knees From Somewhere Inside by Mary Janitch, 1973, 16 x 20 x 12. Reproduced courtesy of Carmen Lamanna Gallery, Toronto.

Mary Janitch's box is surrealistic and gives a hard and soft appearance almost simultaneously. The overall composition suggests a torso without a head. Though all objects used are new, the way in which they have been assembled projects an almost petrified feeling.

The A Hand by Lily Harman. Reproduced courtesy of the artist.

"Collecting old things has always been my vice . . . one day I opened the closet where I'd stowed the treasures and began to arrange the objects . . . I believe in recycling obsolescence . . ."

71

Videotape Structure No. 7 by Colette Whiten, 1972. Reproduced courtesy Carmen Lamanna Gallery, Toronto.

The rigid, almost penal-like apparatus depicted here and on the following pages is used in the process of Colette Whiten's work of plaster casting actual segments of the human body for sculpture purposes. The construction of Colette Whiten's pieces requires immense participation of other people. The whole process is filmed and put on a video tape, and used for documentary purposes at the same time that the construction is on exhibit. The massive wooden open structure—27 feet x 9 feet x 3 feet—forms a box which becomes the main part of the exhibition and moreover serves as a very

private area for the occupants undergoing the process of having parts of their anatomy cast in plaster.

An air or feeling of terror, isolation, sadism and almost ceremonial ritual prevailed throughout the casting. It was caused not only by the tenseness of the occupants due to immobile muscles, or the incongruous tenderness with which the artist and her helpers offered them cigarettes or refreshment while plaster was being mixed or already hardened leg or arm moulds were being removed. It was the entire artistic happening. The scene—in which the box structure serves as a catalyst—suggests the macabre, something of man's historic inhumanity to man and our seeming inability to escape hurting or being hurt by others.

Structure No. 7 (detail) by Colette Whiten, 1972, 67 x 136 x 37. Reproduced courtesy Carmen Lamanna Gallery, Toronto.

The massive structure is a large open box, an area of very private and intimate space for the tied-down occupants, who are undergoing the process of having limbs and parts of their anatomy cast in plaster.

Pages 74 and 75

Structure No. 7 by Colette Whiten, 1972, wood, rope, chain, iron, loops, concrete blocks, 67 x 136 x 37. Reproduced courtesy Carmen Lamanna Gallery, Toronto.

Interplanetary Navigation by Joseph
Cornell, 1964, collage and water-
color, 11⅜ x 8½. Reproduced
courtesy The Solomon R. Guggenheim Museum, gift of Mr. and Mrs.
Walter N. Pharr.

Soft clouds, birds in flight and
angelic figures combine to suggest
a celestial scene.

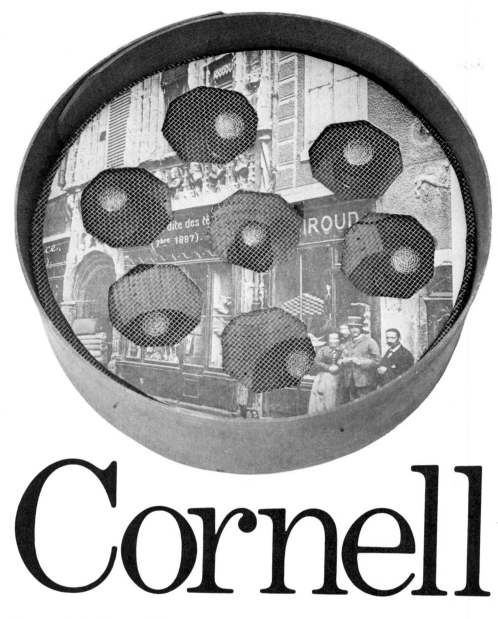

Beehive by Joseph Cornell, 1934, painted wooden box (with lid) containing paper disks, seven metal thimbles, a copper screen and photo-engraving with seven cutouts, 35/8 inches high x 73/4-inch diameter. Collection, The Museum of Modern Art, New York, gift of James Thrall Soby.

Cornell

Strongly influenced by Max Ernst and the Surrealist movement, Joseph Cornell combines everyday objects with old maps and French newspaper clippings in glass-covered boxes to create poetic and often cryptic compositions. For the most part self-taught, Cornell works to achieve a simple serenity out of his remarkable sense of paradox and balance. Secrets, treasures, allegories, astronomy and the heavens, mysteries of past and future, time and space . . . all of these have a presence and a place in Cornell's boxes.

There is something of the juggler and the sleight-of-hand artist in his work, which frequently conveys a spirit of naiveté and sophistication at one and the same time. Cornell projects aspects of the multiple worlds in our yesterdays and tomorrows; strangely missing is the feeling of now. The viewer relates immediately to the innocence and familiarity of the objects used but is bewildered or bewitched by their placement, which often leaves starkly empty areas in the composition, suggesting emotional isolation.

Like pigeons out of a hat, Cornell pulls a seemingly endless array of ideas, sensations and relationships out of his boxes. But there the jesting ends, and the viewer carries away suggestions that sometime later explode in the hidden corners of the mind.

Pantry Ballet for Jacques Offenbach
by Joseph Cornell, 1940, construction, 10½ x 18 x 6. Collection of Mr.
and Mrs. Richard L. Feigen, New
York. Photo by Geoffrey Clements.
Reproduced with kind permission.

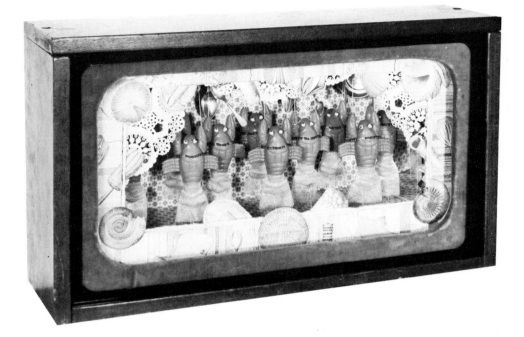

Space Object Box by Joseph Cornell,
construction and collage, 11¹⁄₁₆ x
17⅝ x 5⅜. Reproduced courtesy
The Solomon R. Guggenheim Museum, New York.

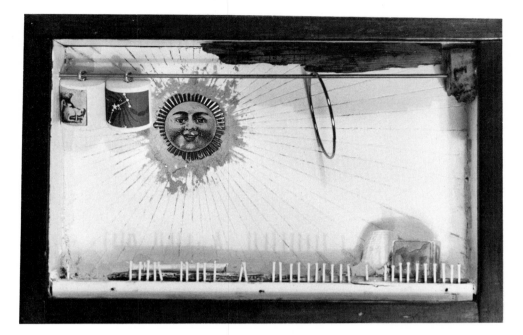

The Sun Box by Joseph Cornell. Reproduced courtesy J. L. Hudson Gallery, Detroit.

Untitled by Joseph Cornell, box with sun, ring and yellow ball, 7⅛ x 11⅛ x 3⅝. Reproduced courtesy Dayton's Gallery 12, Minneapolis.

Night Skies: Auriga by Joseph Cornell, 1954, box containing painted wooden construction with pasted paper, 19¼ x 13½ x 7½. Collection Mr. and Mrs. E. A. Bergman, Chicago. Photograph courtesy the Museum of Modern Art, New York.

Opposite page

Central Park Carrousel—1950, in Memorium by Joseph Cornell, 1950, construction in wood, mirror, wire netting and paper, 20¼ x 14½ x 6¾. Collection, The Museum of Modern Art, New York, Katherine Cornell Fund. Reproduced with kind permission.

Sun Box 1960 by Joseph Cornell. Reproduced courtesy Howard and Jean Lipman, New York. Photo by John D. Schiff.

Hotel Bon Port: Arms in Memory by Joseph Cornell. Reproduced courtesy Mr. and Mrs. E. A. Bergman, Chicago.

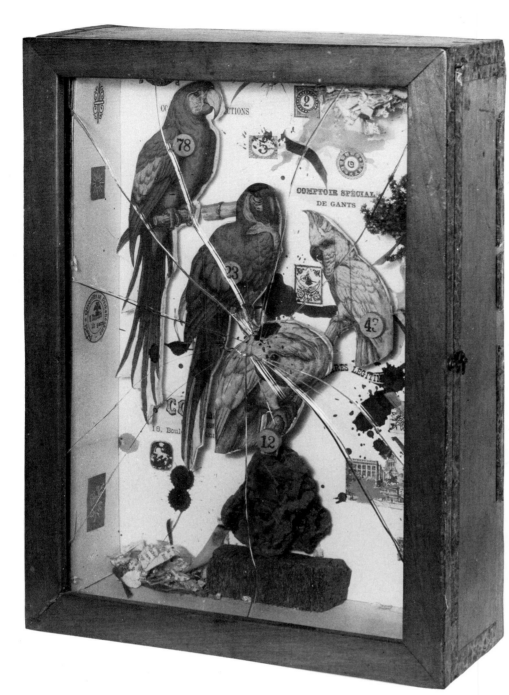

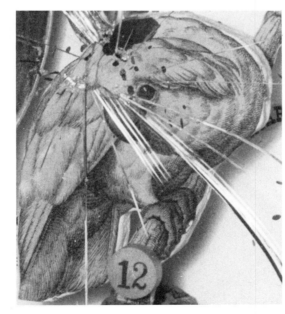

Habitat for a Shooting Gallery (full view and details) by Joseph Cornell, 1943, wooden cabinet containing cutouts of parrots and printed cards, etc., impact-cracked glass. 15½ x 11⅛ x 4¼. Reproduced courtesy Irving Blum, Los Angeles.

Birds are one of Joseph Cornell's favorite themes, perhaps symbolizing the idea of freedom for man and all living things through flight. Here they are caught and numbered under glass.

Taglioni's Jewel Casket by Joseph Cornell, 1940, wooden box containing glass ice cubes, and jewelry, 11 7/8 x 8¼ x 4¾. Collection The Museum of Modern Art, New York, gift of James Thrall Soby. Reproduced with kind permission.

The artist's inscription on the inside lid of the box reads: "On a moonlight night in the winter of 1835 the carriage of Marie Taglioni was halted by a Russian highwayman, and that enchanting creature commanded to dance for this audience of one on a panther's skin spread over the snow beneath the stars. From this actuality arose the legend that to keep alive the memory of this adventure so precious to her, Taglioni formed the habit of placing a piece of artificial ice in her jewel casket or dressing table where, melting among the sparkling stones, there was evoked a hint of the atmosphere of the starlit heavens over the ice-covered landscape."

Red Shoe With Roses from the series *Single Right Men's Shoes* by Gathie Falk, 1973, ceramics, wooden case, varnish. Reproduced courtesy of the artist.

Gathie Falk

"Veneration of the ordinary" is how Gathie Falk describes the allegorical, almost metaphysical imagery she achieves with personal objects such as shoes. By encasement in boxes and layers of plastic, new meaning is given to the things we know so well in other contexts. They become fixed in time, and thus objects of the past, almost like silent memorials to the persons who once might have owned them or known them intimately.

Her sense of juxtaposition is unusually keen—the old is placed beside the new, the baby's shoe stands toe to toe with an adult's, mixtures of unrelated things are combined and suddenly, but with no apparent logic, relate. Gathie Falk's world is one of multiple imagery—running shoes repeat themselves, all facing in the same direction, over and over again, their laces carefully placed, enshrined by application of plastic. Is it a famous explorer's voyage, the death-row criminal's last mile, a walk through a cemetery? It is an iconography created to taunt the viewer's conscience and haunt his memory.

"Looking at my work for several years," she says, "I came to some verbal conclusions about it. I generally make ordinary things like shoes and eggs and shirts and gift boxes with pink ribbons. When I make fruit it is not the exotic pomegranate but apples, oranges, and grapefruit.

"Once made, however, these things are more beautiful than their original models. Often they are put in special places: shrines, glass-doored boxes, cast resin molds. This change from an ordinary household object to a thing that is valued and honored has sometimes been called a *veneration of the ordinary*.

"I like to work mostly in clay because it allows me to make objects that have soft undulating surfaces like living flesh. I like to choose from the real world only those details that seem significant to the sculpture, and add to that whatever pleases me that is surreal or fanciful. For instance, the shoes, in shape, are fairly realistic, but a row of eighteen pairs of dark red shoes with rose decals in the heels and a strawberry inside one of them is not a sight run into very often.

"While I do not like to impose limits on the possibilities of the work I am going to do, I still choose very carefully what is (and how it is) done. The general belief that it is all just a lot of fun is fictitious."

Preserved Shoes, Living Room Series by Gathie Falk, 1968, ceramics, polyester resin. Reproduced courtesy of the artist.

The shoes are almost like a memorial, and radiate an unreal, ghostlike presence.

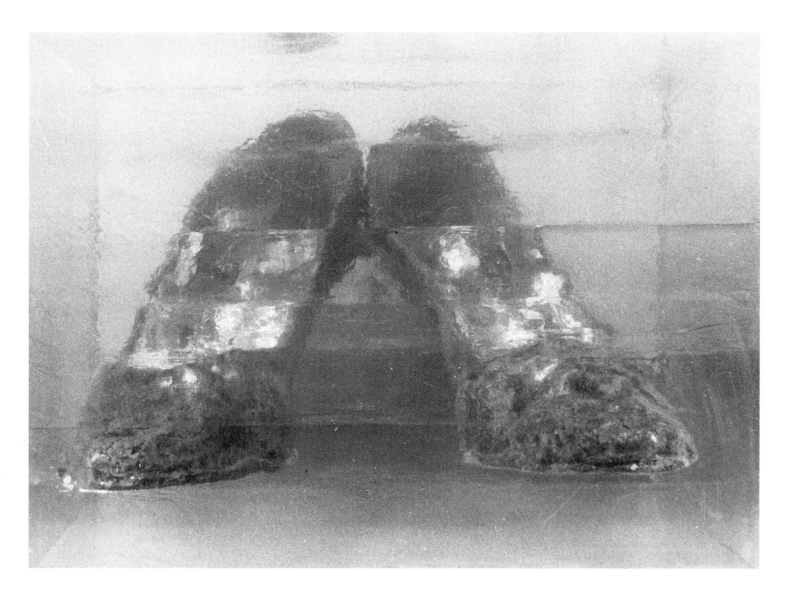

Bird Cage, Living Room Series by Gathie Falk, 1971, ceramics and bird cage. Reproduced courtesy of the artist.

Four Half Apples by Gathie Falk, 1971, ceramics, acrylics, polyester resin and Plexiglas. Collection Millie McKibbon. Reproduced with kind permission.

"I use down-to-earth apples, grapefruit and oranges . . . each piece has a blossom and stem, a beginning and an end."

Pages 88 and 89

Both box compositions are entitled: *Two Shoes With Roses*. From the series *Single Right Men's Shoes* by Gathie Falk, 1972, ceramics, roses, varnish, paint, wooden case, mirror and nail polish. Reproduced courtesy of the artist.

The shoes in the cabinet on page 88 are ghostly outlines, the roses indiscernible. Is the glass a mirror reflecting something elusive behind you, or has it been opaqued by the passage of time to show you in it only what you are most desperately trying to remember?

Six Orange Brogues from the series *Single Right Men's Shoes* by Gathie Falk, 1973, ceramics, wooden case, varnish. Reproduced courtesy the artist.

Clay, glaze, paint, varnish, found objects, fabric, pen drawing on paper, pen drawing on clay, pencil drawing, oil paint or acrylic paint on clay, block on clay, fabric, wood, wood (clouds) painted with acrylic paint and varnished, Plexiglas and polyester resin are among the materials used by Gathie Falk to create her boxes.

*Six Black Patent Leather Boots and
Eight Blue Runners* both from the
series *Single Right Men's Shoes* by
Gathie Falk, 1973, ceramics, wooden
case and varnish. Reproduced
courtesy of the artist.

A Child's View of Shelley by Varujan Boghosian, 1969, tin, wood, and iron, 16 x 14 x 4½. Reproduced courtesy of the artist.

While Falk creates memorials through her treatment of a single object, Boghosian uses the grouping of a number of items to establish a mood of *in memoriam*. In *A Child's View of Shelley*, Boghosian's objects are traditional death symbols: the severed hand which is many times seen at the top of a tombstone pointing to heaven, the cruciform design, the nail which is an allusion to death on the cross. The composition is commemorative of votive folk images seen in some Spanish and Mexican churches.

Objects

Many artists working with boxes seek to change the basic format or shape of the box by adding things to it, painting on it, marking or scoring it, or trying to change it or the objects in it with various artistic techniques and treatments. Other artists insert objects into the box without changing them. The characteristics of the container frequently determine the size, shape and nature of these objects, which in turn affect the original box. When the objects are recognizable, familiar, everyday items, they may not be artistically important by themselves, but through their positioning with other objects new relationships are evolved, and the composition assumes significance. In this sense, assemblage is very important to the box artist.

In *Searcher* by James Seawright and *A Quintessent Notion* by Amy Brown (see page 98), a bell-shaped jar and bird cage are used; both are similar in shape and size and still both pieces of work project entirely different moods and feelings. None of the objects used in either composition has been tampered with or changed; they are what they always were. It is the manner in which they have been placed in relationship to each other that creates a forceful environment. They all work together.

In essence, a box is a box as long at it *contains*, no matter what the shape. Its shape represents a challenge to the artist to make it aesthetic, dynamic, radical, simple or complex through inserting items and objects which, alone or together, fascinate and communicate.

I Remember Papa by David McManaway, 1964, mixed media, 5¾ high. Collection Paul Rogers Harris. Photo by Hence Griffith. Reproduced with kind permission.

The 5 Highs by George Herms, 1960,
assemblage, 24¾ x 10⅜ x 5½.
Reproduced courtesy Pasadena Art
Museum, Betty and Monte Factor
Family Collection. Photo by Frank J.
Thomas.

This box, relief in nature, has the
quality of being like an artist's
atelier arrayed with the objects he
or she would use to create a still-life
composition. It is an assemblage of
things placed in random disarrange-
ment; yet each somehow manages
to relate to the others. The viewer
sees a rusty chain, a gum-ball
machine, an egg in a nest, an old
bracelet, a piece of reflective material,
a dirty cloud made of soiled cotton,
a part of a doll, a hank of hair and
numerous other objects all related to a
soiled, worn and discolored flag at the
foundation of the box. The box shape
has not been tampered with but the
treatment of the objects suggests
a Kafka-esque world, perhaps
Amerika.

Right. The Puddle by Sherry Grayner, reproduced courtesy Department of External Affairs, Ottawa. The metal containers have been coated with a plastic-like substance which gives a ghostlike effect and transforms them into pillow-soft objects.

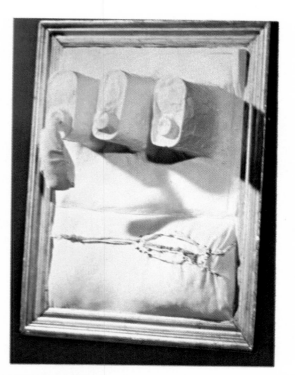

Left and center. Box constructions by Leslie Logue, painting, mirrored aluminum and Plexiglas. These highly polished constructions, encased in plastic boxes of varying shapes, use refracted light and attributes of transparency with great effectiveness.

Right. Cup in Box by Ron Nagle, 1968, ceramic, wood and plastic; cup is 3 inches high. Courtesy Objects: U. S. A., The Johnson Collection of Contemporary Crafts.

A highly polished, almost erotic-looking clay cup is the principal figure in this box. Punctured and perforated, it is unusable as a cup; encased in a box and isolated from everything else, it becomes an aesthetic artifact.

Left. Installation Brand, boxes by John Schroeder, 1971.

Center. Death of the Laced Ones by John Schroeder, 1972.

Right. Untitled by John Schroeder, 1972. Reproduced courtesy of the artist.

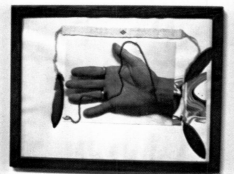

"Most of the materials that I use are natural. I try to combine elements into a greater whole. The most important work to me is that which sort of 'passes through.' It is like an image picture that flashes into 'reality'. The problem then is to figure out the logistics of putting together the piece. I use the colors of the Oglala Sioux for their symbolic properties, and certain of the objects for the same reasons: a sea-bird feather for flight and the sea; a shell of a certain kind to denote a specific geographic location; a star for time, space, and knowledge; and so forth, so that each object chosen adds harmoniously to the parts of the whole through its symbolic and spiritual qualities."

Searcher by James Seawright, 1966, metal, plastic and electronic parts, 53¾ x 20 x 20. Collection Whitney Museum of American Art, New York, gift of the Howard and Jean Lipman Foundation, Inc. Photo by Geoffrey Clements.

A Quintessant Notion by Amy Brown, 1973. Reproduced courtesy of the artist.

These two boxes, appearing so similar, are opposites in their materials and artistic spirit. James Seawright's composition is a 20th-century, and even futuristic, concept; metal and transparent materials suggest science, space and time. Amy Brown's bird nest, eggs and bare fish spine are cushioned in an organic past, set on a circlet of fur which softens the decayed and ancient effect of the composition. The Brown box looks back to when living things prevailed; Seawright's effort points toward a technological tomorrow.

Opposite page

The Spectators by Gordon Wagner, 1971. Collection Mr. and Mrs. S. Fishman. Reproduced with kind permission.

This box has a gaudy, turn-of-the-century look about it, reminiscent of a trip to Coney Island or some fondly remembered amusement park.

Skins of Us by Walter Nottingham, crocheted wool, rayon, horsehair mounted on velvet platform, Plexiglas box, 16 x 66 x 30. Reproduced courtesy the Museum of Contemporary Crafts, New York, from Sculpture in Fiber exhibition, 1972. Photo by Bob Hanson.

There is a mummy-like effect to this box, even though the ornate casket has been replaced by a completely transparent box. The viewer is in direct confrontation with an emaciated figure whose life-line seems to extend beyond the tomb in macabre strands of material which seem to be leaking out of the box.

· *Box* by Robert Filliou. Reproduced courtesy of the artist.

"Open your mind to all life and not merely yours . . . open your mind to all art not merely mine . . . don't close your mind to this piece and and you will like it . . ."

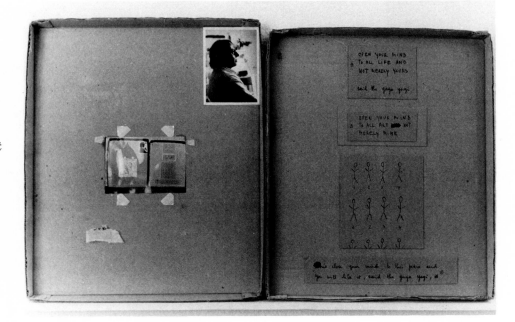

Below, left. Memorabilia Self-Portrait No. 3 by Bob Camblin, wax, skull, nails, boxes and secret-rolled-up message in wooden box, 9 x 4. Collection Dianne David, Houston. Photo by Rodney Susholtz.

"My boxes and compositions are autobiographical in that I have now lived about 24 million minutes and the works relate to some of these experiences. They are a bit like snakeskin after the snake has grown and moved on."

Below, right. Magic Set by Robert Hedrick. Reproduced courtesy Morris Gallery, Toronto.

Hedrick's unique shapes and objects are sculpted of bronze and displayed much like jewelery on trays and in boxes that are mirrored or velvet lined. Don't you have an immediate impulse to change the order of the arrangement? Positioning and the play of shape against shape is an integral part of this composition.

Ancient music box decorated with oil crayon and shellac by Norman Laliberté. Photo by Thecla.

This old music box now has a tune for the eyes as well as the ears— a home-sweet-home scene in one of the panelling depressions. Doves, flowers and frilly objects have been affixed at another level to heighten the feeling of depth and to add a touch of sentimentality to the machine. Despite the decor, one gets the feeling that the machine really doesn't work; the added decorative and nostalgic composition is all that remains of its former musical charm.

Yaddo-Egg Box by Ilse Getz, 1958,
14 x 14. Collection Iris Clert.
Reproduced courtesy of the artist.

Folk art, memories, the oppression
of European history are all among
components, visible and spiritual,
of the boxes created by Ilse Getz.
She places pieces of doll anatomy
and other objects within her boxes
at a point where the emptiness of
the environment—the sparseness of
objects coupled with strategic
positioning—will reach its highest
pitch.

The Observer by Amy Brown, 1969,
24 x 21 x 45. Reproduced courtesy
of the artist.

Vestiges of modern man's existence
are juxtaposed with a doleful,
human eye, while the box, covered
in black lace, creates a mood of
mourning. The almost unrecognize-
able objects used in the composition,
coupled with the photograph of the
early motor vehicle, suggest a time
and place rapidly vanishing from
memory.

Poéme en prose by Daniel Spoerri, 1960. Reproduced courtesy Galleria Schwarz, Milan.

The box is like a table on which an accumulation of dishes and effects suggests a difficult period which its occupant may have been undergoing.

Perhaps he or she was a writer and the table debris traces the sheer physical dilemma of thoughts being transformed into words. The cigarette butts, crushed paper, and cherry pits reveal that it wasn't an easy birth.

Daniel Spoerri's boxes, which are exhibited as wall-hangings, are composed as though purely by chance. His objects, glued in place, resemble vignettes and situations out of daily life. There is a "stop camera" appearance about them, as if the occupant were present but an instant ago, and now has vanished into thin air.

No. 18 Egg by Irene Whittome, 1969, assemblage, 30 x 34 x 9½. Reproduced courtesy Galerie Martal, Montreal.

"My art forms from collecting cast-off materials, photographs for imagery, and waste either bought or reproduced, and placing these *unrelated materials* into boxes.

"Within these enclosed dimensions the space is compressed by stuffing in waste up to the glass pane, or the objects interact openly by being glued or hung on rods. The repetitive presentation of the objects in the interior as well as the exterior—several boxes containing the same object—is very important.

"I incorporate as many highly contrasting materials as possible, glass with cotton waste, chrome with cotton batting, rope with plaster, photographs in plastic bags, etc.

"The essential is only the forming. Through the process, the form is created."

Top. Chiropractor's Wife by May Wilson. Reproduced courtesy of the artist.

When you move to a new house, apartment or city, you place your most precious possessions in one box and virtually guard it with your life. May Wilson's box portrays this tender but fierce emotion.

Center. Dog Star by D. E. Shaw, 1972, wood, cloth, metal and bone, 28 x 14 x 10. Reproduced courtesy Dianne David, Houston. Photo by John Bintliff.

D. E. Shaw creates ". . . small poems in an effort to embrace the monumental." His *Dog Star* box seems to have a number of fleeting elements, a column of hearts, a lace tablecloth, a painting of young people looking towards the horizon, a small hand perhaps grasping for life.

Bottom. Panorama Machine by Richard Prince, 1972, wood, plastic, metal and photographs, 6 x 6 x 3. Reproduced courtesy of the artist.

Turn the handle and the village scene depicted in the *Panorama Machine* comes to life.

"I consider myself to be working with the landscape or perhaps more generally with the environment . . . The box functions as a vision-directing device as well as a filter. In many cases it serves to isolate the object from the rest of the surrounding space and so direct the vision and the thought of the spectator into that other space you have created. In other instances it functions as a filter."

Above. I Love You by Ronna Mogelon. Reproduced courtesy of the artist. Photo by Larry Mogelon.

Silver hearts, pieces cut from a paper doily and popcorn prizes set in a plastic soap box create a child's valentine.

Left. La vielle boite (The old box) by Irene Whittome, 1969/70, 20 x 27 x 7. Reproduced courtesy of the artist.

The spheres are like eyes peering out of dark apertures in eyeball to eyeball confrontation with the viewer. One has the feeling that the audience (and not the work of art) is on exhibition.

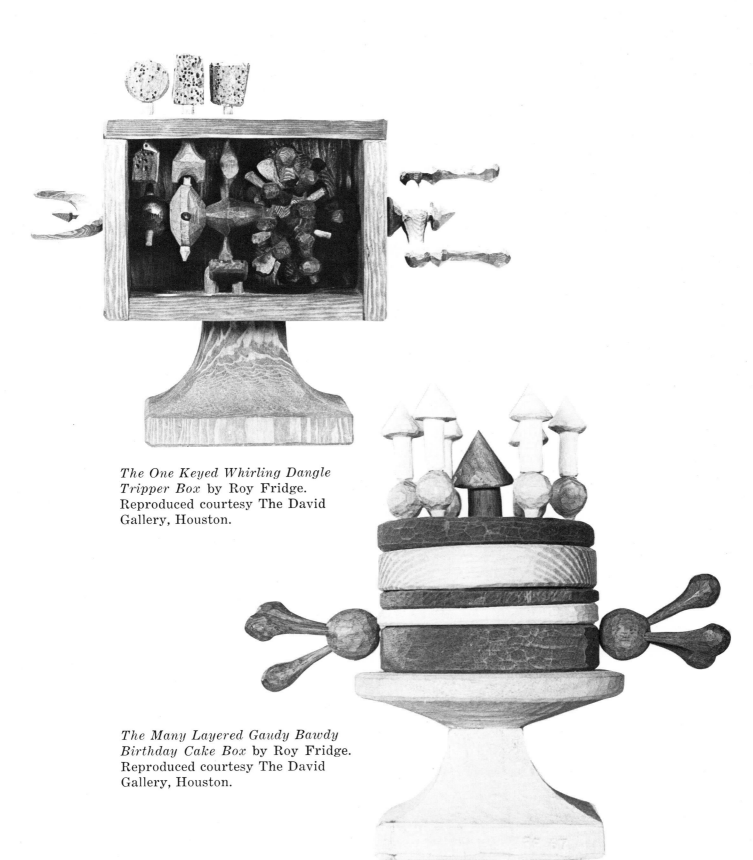

The One Keyed Whirling Dangle Tripper Box by Roy Fridge. Reproduced courtesy The David Gallery, Houston.

The Many Layered Gaudy Bawdy Birthday Cake Box by Roy Fridge. Reproduced courtesy The David Gallery, Houston.

The *Many Layered Gaudy Bawdy Birthday Cake Box* looks as if it were made of candy with candles (or are they rockets?) perched on top. The *One Keyed Whirling Dangle Tripper Box* seems to be composed of a maze of pieces humorously interlocked and reminiscent of something out of the Stone Age. Both pieces seem to have many moving parts, which appear to really work.

Roy Fridge feels that "a box is a reliquary . . . a theater . . . a museum or just a controlled place to put things. It is mysterious and magic." He adds, "A box is a box, a room, a temple, shrine or all the world. I am a part-time hermit and an elective rustic who whittles. I make what I call Low Art—corny, romantic, folk-primitive. Unfortunately I am too sophisticated to be primitive . . . but I try."

Left. Phoebe Rising by David McManaway, 1971, mixed media, 53 inches high. Collection Pete and Lesley Schlumberger, Houston. Photo courtesy Paul Rogers Harris, Dallas, taken by Hickey and Robertson.

Right. Heart Box by David McManaway, 1971, 20⅛ x 6½ x 3⅞. Collection Mr. and Mrs. Joseph Hirshhorn. Photo courtesy Paul Rogers Harris, Dallas.

David McManaway's boxes and constructions are an unusual combination of the child-like and the highly sophisticated. He has little regard for order, balance or systematizing. His primary concern is that whatever he places within his composition (and wherever he places it) has something to do with the idea he is conveying to the viewer. He works with bought and found objects to produce the imaginary, the sentimental and the contemporary.

The objects and things which he collects and lives with have more than a physical presence—they are his language of communication. He considers art more of a game than actual work; when he works (or plays) he thinks of himself and of his favorite people, and aspects of his and their lives emerge in his art.

115

Private Joko by David McManaway,
1967, construction, 25 x 12 x 5.
Collection Paul Rogers Harris.
Photo by Harry Bennett.
Reproduced with kind permission.

An unusual collection of faces and
what appear to be cloth bundles
(together with a solitary flower)
have been pigeonholed to form this
rather haunting pedestaled box-
composition. McManaway speaks of
the "visual touch," the ability to find
the right thing at the right time
and to position it in the right place.
"I will not make a composition,"
he says, "unless I get this particular
awareness, and it is always right.
I trust it. I find things in this same
manner. My search for objects gives
me an excuse for traveling about.
The whole operation would seem to
be a rather silly business these
days, but it is the only one that
interests me."

A box construction by Louise Nevelson. Reproduced courtesy The J. L. Hudson Gallery, Detroit.

Louise Nevelson

Louise Nevelson's boxes are carefully composed with a monumentality that creates great intellectual and, at the same time, emotional impact. Consisting of often-standardized architectural and furniture moldings, as well as found wooden construction objects, each box she assembles nevertheless has its own unique style. Brought together and mounted in series, the boxes maintain their individuality while contributing in a precise way to the dynamics of the whole or greater composition. Black or gold paint is frequently used to unify the over-all work and to highlight the varying textures and grains of the countless pieces and blocks of wood.

Nevelson's found wooden materials are a virtual carpentry shop: posts, pillars, legs, wooden discs, dowels, pegs, arms, seats, cylinders, finials, balusters, newels, splats—all of these in varying styles, sizes and shapes find their way into her boxes. There is a divine precision to her work that somehow engulfs the viewer in an attitude of mysticism. Fascinated by the varying textural surfaces, intrigued by the play of shape against shape, overwhelmed by the impact of box upon box, he contemplates the absolute and irrevocable statement that has been made.

Cryptics XXV (closed view) by
Louise Nevelson, painted black
wood, 8 x 8. Reproduced courtesy
The J. L. Hudson Gallery, Detroit.

Night Flight I by Louise Nevelson,
1972, painted black wood, 84 x 125 x
7½. Collection Seattle Airport.
Reproduced courtesy Pace Gallery,
New York. Photo by William Suttle.

118

Dawn Tide by Louise Nevelson, 1960, gold painted wood, 85¾ x 37¾ x 9⁹⁄₁₆. Reproduced courtesy Pace Gallery, New York.

Royal Tide I by Louise Nevelson, 1960, gold painted wood, 96 x 36. Collection Howard and Jean Lipman, New York. Photo by Rudolph Burckhardt. Reproduced with kind permission.

Opposite page

Details from *Royal Tide I* by Louise Nevelson.

Page 122

Luminous Zag by Louise Nevelson, 1971, black painted wood, 96 x 76 x 10, (36 boxes on 18-inch base). Reproduced courtesy Pace Gallery, New York. Photo by William Suttle.

Page 123

Black Crescent Wall by Louise Nevelson, 1971, black painted wood, 133½ x 86 x 11, (48 boxes on 12 inch base). Reproduced courtesy Pace Gallery, New York.

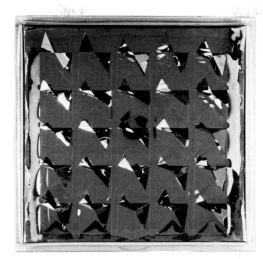

Reflections by Michael Michaeledes, clear acrylic box frame with wooden backboard, supporting cut and creased three-dimensional reflective surface made of silver Mylar (metal and plastic laminate), 14½ x 14½ x 3. Reproduced courtesy Alecto International, London and New York.

Multiples

By taking a simple and sometimes quite insignificant object and repeating it graphically—as in a printed image, by repetitive organization or by multiplication—the artist is able to evoke responses to the object that lie dormant within the viewer when he faces the original object in its single or individual entity. Ordinarily an eye is an eye, but through sheer repetition a new visual pattern is created, leaving the viewer somewhat perplexed, engrossed and responsible for finding a meaningful explanation.

The box camera (see page 6) has been used over and over again as a simple instrument to reproduce as many images as available film would allow. In *Clic, Clac, Kodak, Hourrah* (see page 129) Arman (Armand Fernandez) has depicted with great impact the box camera's obsolescence. The individual camera is merely old; almost identical cameras, arranged in multiples, portray more than age, they constitute a junk-heap of time.

Through multiples a dynamic impact is communicated, and new arrangements, new entities and new concepts are indelibly registered in the mind. In *Arteriosclerose* (see page 128) we see multiples of forks and spoons which individually are very formal, personal and dignified utensils. Thrown together in seemingly pell-mell disorder their dignity is lost and we become conscious of the hundreds of thousands of people who every day use the same cutlery as we ourselves do. In a somewhat similar vein, *Valetudinarian* (see page 131) confronts the viewer with a staggering sight—an avalanche of pill bottles. We cannot help but be impressed, and perhaps alarmed, by our growing dependence on drugs and other pharmaceutical products.

Opposite page

Work Brass 402, No. 15, Series A by Aiko Miyawaki, 1966, 46 x 46 x 7. Collection The Solomon R. Guggenheim Museum, New York. Photo courtesy Tokyo Gallery, Tokyo, taken by H. Nakano.

Miyawaki's mosaic wall journeys in all directions. Though the viewer is not quite sure of its actual dimensions, the instant impression is that it is huge, its massiveness broken by a series of square and rectangular openings. The wall is made up of hundreds of small box-like cubes which become highly effective through controlled lighting playing upon the wall's transparencies.

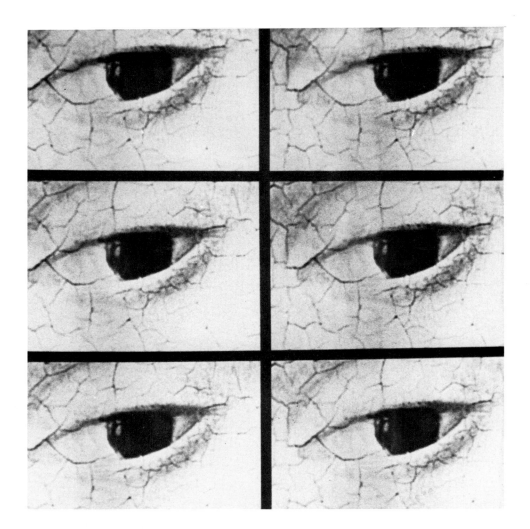

Box Construction (detail) by Irene Whittome. Reproduced courtesy of the artist.

The eyes are like a Renaissance painting aged by time. Their multiplication produces a mythological air of a spirit that sees all and knows all.

Opposite page

Stone Group by Mary Bauermeister, 1964, stones, 24 x 24. Reproduced courtesy The Aldrich Museum, Ridgefield, Conn., and Galeria Bonino Ltd., New York. Photo by Lise Steiner.

Pebbles, grains of sand, pieces of earth, driftwood, found objects, old pieces of torn cloth, all enlarged or distorted by the power of magnifying glass lenses and juxtaposed with drawings or paintings of these same found objects, are the materials that form many of Mary Bauermeister's box compositions.

The result is a many-faceted perspective on these relief objects, a view that is dependent on the stance and nearness of the viewer to produce images which are capable of journeying into infinity.

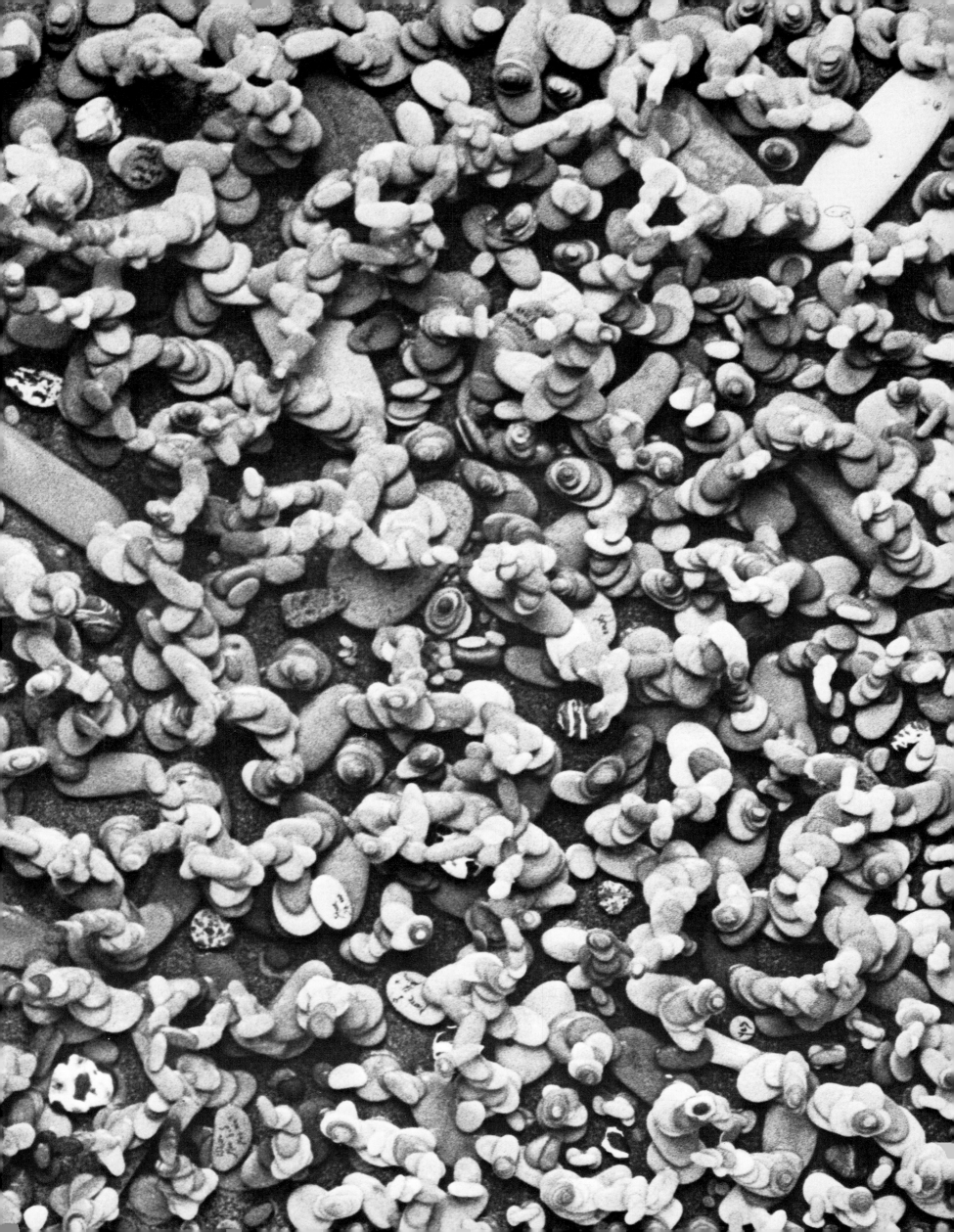

Above. Untitled by Arman (Armand Fernandez) 1960, plastic water pistols in Plexiglas case, 8¼ x 23¼ x 4½. Collection The Museum of Modern Art, New York, gift of Philip Johnson. Reproduced with kind permission.

Right. Artériosclérose by Arman, 1961, forks and spoons in a glass covered box, 18¼ x 28⅝ x 3. Collection Galleria Schwarz, Milan. Photo by Bacci. Reproduced with kind permission.

A member of the French "New Realism" movement, which was particularly active in the early 1960s, Armand Fernandez is best known for his accumulations of identical objects housed in boxes, which have an explosive impact on the viewer. Arman is conscious of the contemporary tendency to ". . . flood our world with junk and odd objects . . ." in the process of bringing progress through mass consumption and, subsequently, mass obsolescence. He believes that his art serves to resurrect these rejected objects, bringing new dignity to them by raising them to the level of an art composition.

Opposite page

Above. Clic, Clac, Kodak, Hourrah by Arman, 1963, 20 x 29 x ¾. Reproduced courtesy Locksley/Shea Gallery, Minneapolis.

Below. Untitled (F) by Stephen Posen, 1971, acrylic and oil on canvas, 78 x 38. Reproduced courtesy Virginia Museum of Fine Arts, Richmond, Virginia.

An actual full-size cloth and box construction served as a model for this composition. The artist considers the construction of the boxes and cloth model as a vital part of the painting. ". . . Whatever emotional choice is made in taking a photograph, I make that choice when I select the cloth, when I select the color, when I build the arrangement of boxes. When those boxes are built, every choice that I can foresee is already decided, and in a sense the painting is made at that point . . . the painting is the same size as the structure. It is a one-to-one kind of relationship . . ."

« La beauté n'est que la promesse du bonheur. » (Stendhal.)

Page 130
Glou-Glou (Bis) by Arman, 1961.
Collection Galleria Schwarz, Milan.
Photo by Bacci. Reproduced with
kind permission.

Page 131
Valetudinarian by Arman, 1960,
pill bottles in a painted wood and
glass case, 16 x 23¾ x 3⅛. Collec-
tion The Museum of Modern Art,
New York, gift of Philip Johnson.
Photo by Rudolph Burckhardt.
Reproduced with kind permission.

Collective Memory by Fred Otnes.
Reproduced courtesy of the artist.

An old type-case drawer has been
segmented into a series of compartments, each of which represents a
visual chapter in the story of a
people. The field-flower cutting
suggests a note of hope in sadness.

Vrindaban by Octavia Paz.
Reproduced courtesy Éditions
Claude Givaudan, Geneva.

Divisions, grids and type cases

In the section dealing with multiples, we have illustrated how organized or disorderly arrangements of common, everyday objects can create new patterns that succeed in defining themselves within the over-all box composition, and casually or formally divide the space among themselves. In this section, artists deliberately create divisions, dividing and re-dividing their space so that a spirit of organization may prevail.

Purely functional instruments and machines become works of art unintentionally because of divisions upon divisions, grids upon grids (see page 135). Often the work of art is far from secondary or accidental but instead emerges from functional materials cleverly manipulated to become a series of divisions or boxes (see page 136). Purely artistic works may have a functional look about them. Roger Vilder's *Homage to Constructivism No. 4* serves almost as a simple blueprint for Sol LeWitt's *Untitled (Open Modular Cube)*, both on page 138, which is a series of three-dimensional complex divisions. Soto succeeds in creating apparently simple linear areas (*Untitled*, page 144) by dividing his space with stretched, horizontal wires. Compare this to Sue Fuller's *String Composition* (page 144), where orderly precision yields results that are rhythmical and full of movement.

133

Overall-view of the International
Business Machines Corporation's A
Computer Perspective, an exhibition
on the development of computer
science created by the office of
Charles and Ray Eames (see
page 13). Reproduced courtesy
I.B.M. Corporation, Charles and
Ray Eames and the Howard
University Press.

A series of boxes and grids, set at
varying levels and depths,
chronologically depict the history of
the development of the computer
sciences. The boxes serve to isolate
the viewer's attention so that
concentration on one particular
aspect or phase of computer history
may be achieved within the flow of
the whole story.

The Whirlwind 1 Computer, 1940.
Reproduced courtesy I.B.M.
Corporation.

Myriad electronic parts, wires and
pieces of equipment are arranged in
a series of multiple divisions and
grids to create an apparatus capable
of achieving equally complex results.
This computer, conceived to
simulate or monitor air traffic
and/or industrial-process control,
resembles a large and intriguing
box construction.

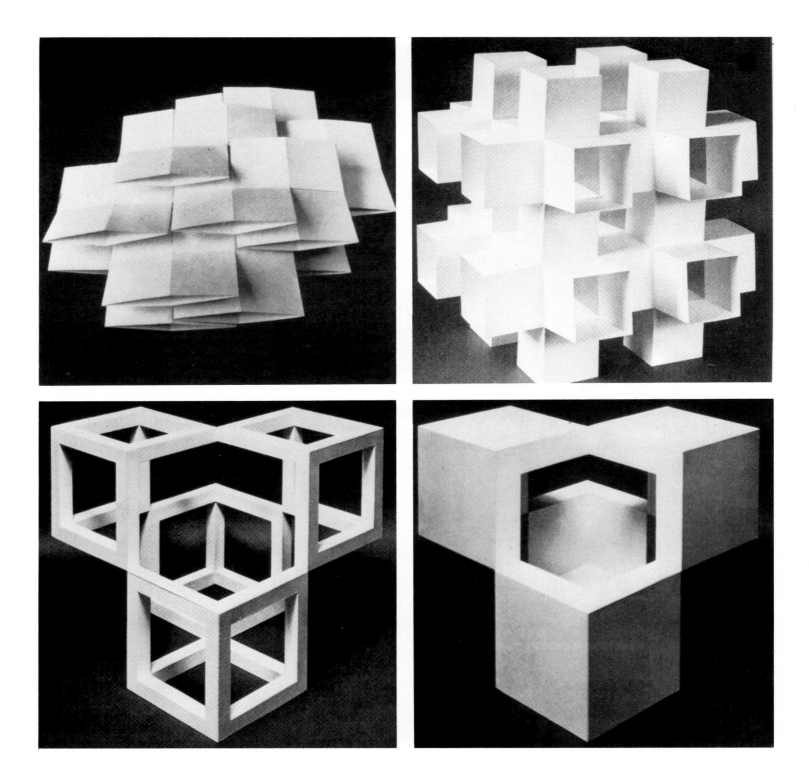

Paper box constructions by Kurt Londenberg. Reproduced courtesy Scherpe Verlag, Germany, publishers of *Papier und Form*.

Top left. Flattened, flexible paper form.

Top right. Flattened form yields a three-dimensional series of stacked boxes.

Bottom left and right. Variations of the box form in the paper construction medium.

Though the work depicted may appear as a kind of paper sculpture, these constructions and forms have much practical application in architecture and industrial design, specifically in the study of form, structure, and space, and their relationships to each other.

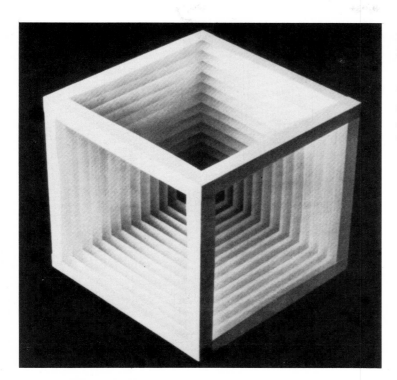

A cube by Kurt Londenberg. Reproduced courtesy of Scherpe Verlag, Germany.

This construction of folded strips demonstrates continuity of structure and strength of three-dimensional organization.

Tesseract, an extensible geometric mobile based on the Four Dimensional Cube, designed and manufactured by Kaufman Designers Company, New York, copyright 1972 by Eyton Kaufman, New York. Reproduced with kind permission.

When viewed from different angles, the mobile changes configurations; its colors alternate continuously between white and black, creating a constant stream of new relationships between color and shape.

Construction (detail) by Roger Vilder. Reproduced courtesy The Electric Gallery, Toronto.

Untitled (detail) by Sol LeWitt, 1966, open modular cube, painted wood, 72 x 72 x 72. Reproduced courtesy John Weber Gallery, New York.

Homage to Constructivism No. 4 by Roger Vilder, 1971, steel, arborite, motor, 42 x 42 x 8. Reproduced courtesy The Electric Gallery, Toronto.

Untitled (detail) by Tim Lambert, 1972, acrylic on polyethylene, two sections, 96 x 120. Reproduced courtesy The Aldrich Museum, Ridgefield, Conn.

These four examples range from Roger Vilder's simple but effective criss-cross or flat tic-tac-toe pattern to the more complex modular three-dimensional boxes of Sol LeWitt. In Roger Vilder's *Construction*, light has been carefully placed to create division within division, while Tim Lambert's *Untitled* box has been encased in reflective plastic sheeting to achieve added effects.

138

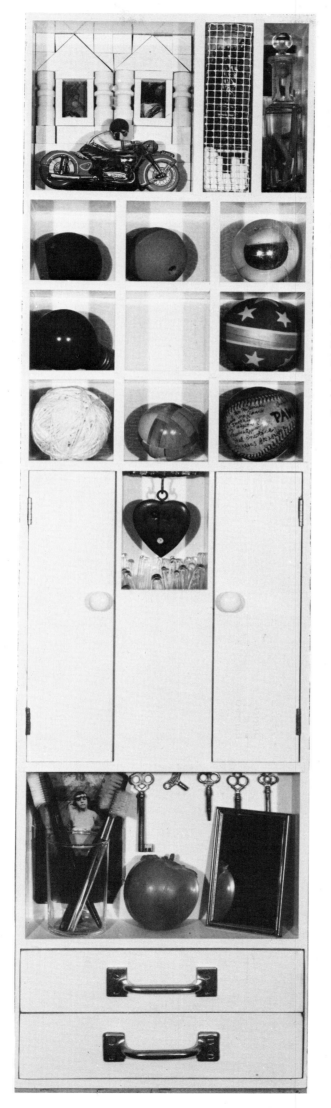

Repository by George Brecht, 1961, wall cabinet with miscellaneous small objects, 40⅜ x 10½ x 3⅛. Collection The Museum of Modern Art, New York, Larry Aldrich Foundation Fund. Reproduced with kind permission.

Among the objects contained in the cabinet are a tennis ball, a pocket watch, a thermometer, balls made of both rubber and plastic, a baseball, a statuette, a wooden puzzle and items such as tooth brushes, bottle caps, pencils, coins, keys, photographs, playing cards, a dollar bill and even a fossilized worm. Such unrelated objects stored in an ordinary cabinet containing divisions and grids reflect the artist's personality, evoking the image of himself which he wants to project. The many round items play against the linear shape of the cabinet, while the doors and drawers serve to divide the space even further.

Work No. 9, 1939, New York by
Charles Biederman, painted wood
and glass. Reproduced courtesy of
the artist.

A pure and simple system of grids
serves to divide the box in length,
width and depth. The result is highly
sophisticated and a pleasant visual
treat. The viewer's original impulse
is to place things on the ledges and
within the various divisions, but
then he begins to admire the artist's
discipline in restricting himself to
pure construction.

140

8' Balance Exposed, Guarded and Enclosed by Michael Craig-Martin, 1970, wood, wire, mesh, mild steel and lead, 30 x 144. Reproduced courtesy Rowan Gallery, London. Photo by John Webb, FRPS.

The artist creates a number of effects —visible, invisible, transparent, opaque—in this triptych type of box. Its compositional strength lies in diagonals that segment rectangles, thus heightening spatial interest.

Work No. 5, 1937, Paris by Charles Biederman. Reproduced courtesy of the artist.

Another example of Biederman's simple and pure approach to producing a box of great appeal and sophistication.

Right. Study for Hermes by Varujan Boghosian, 1973, wood, steel and glass, 24¾ x 19 x 3½. Reproduced courtesy of Cordier & Ekstrom, Inc., New York.

This is a most elegant box with its play of varying wood textures and array of highly polished spheres embedded within the wood itself. The rainbow-like sphere in the center acts as if it were the gnomon of a sundial, opening up areas of light on the countenance of the cabinet.

Below. Wunderkinder (detail) by Ilse Getz, 1970, 32¼ x 16⅝. Reproduced courtesy of the artist.

The artist has isolated the doll figure within a series of chambers. The figure would be isolated even outside its prison, for it is limbless.

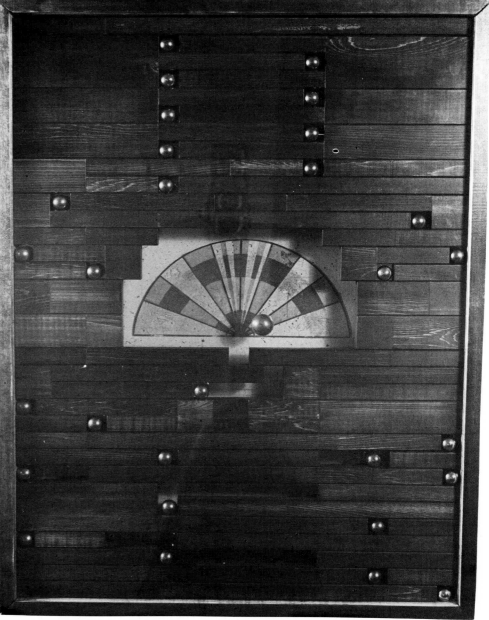

Collection by Janet Palmer, 1973. Reproduced courtesy of the artist. Photo by Bob Palmer.

An ordinary printer's type case for monotype serves as a repository for photographs, shells, type faces, lead soldiers, cards, small bottles—a visual dictionary of fond memory.

142

House of Flowers by Ilse Getz, 1958, 16 x 14. Reproduced courtesy Galleria Schwartz, Milan. Photo by Evelyn Hofer.

The figures depicted seem battered and forlorn; the candles are like memorials to what they once were. In speaking of her box constructions, Ilse Getz says, "Almost twenty years ago I made my first box construction. It became an infinitive process of building, of putting together, of fixing found objects in space. It became an exciting diversion and challenge from my painting and collages, where the problems are similar but quite different from working with found objects and things which we have in everyday life . . . In the beginning the old worn boxes and the perfection and purity of the egg (see *Yaddo Egg Box,* page 106) became a necessary statement . . . The doll, the bird, the game-board, playing cards, clock faces and other objects were added later . . . Much of my time is spent looking for my materials at New England flea markets and antique shops. Sometimes these objects remain for years in my studio before I am able to use them . . ."

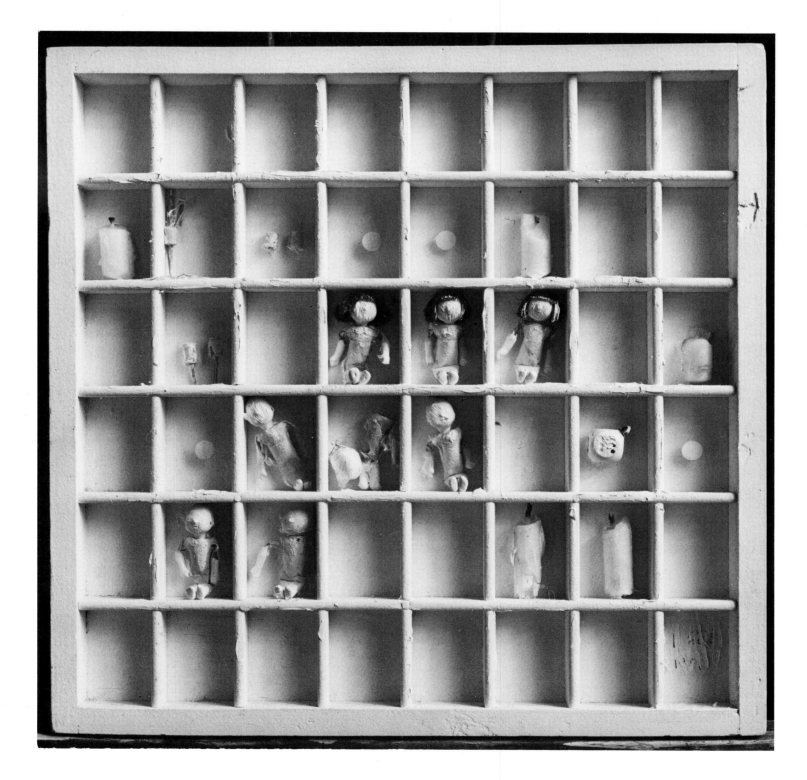

Untitled (Edition Mat) by Soto, 1965, painted wood box with a vertical wire, 18½ x 5 x 11½. Reproduced courtesy Multiples Inc., New York. Photo by Nathan Rabin.

Vibrations by Soto, 1967, white box with silkscreen on the inside rear panel and a Plexiglas front panel, 12½ x 17 x 3½. Reproduced courtesy Multiples Inc., New York. Photo by Nathan Rabin.

String Composition No. T-220 by Sue Fuller, 1965, synthetic fibers, 42 x 42. Collection Marion Koogler McNay Art Institute, San Antonio, gift of Emerson Crocker. Reproduced with kind permission.

All three of these boxes are divided and subdivided with string and wire, which serve to create infinite possibilities. The string and wire can be interlaced or overlapped to give birth to an endless array of secondary patterns and grids, just as paper is used in the Paz box on page 133.

144

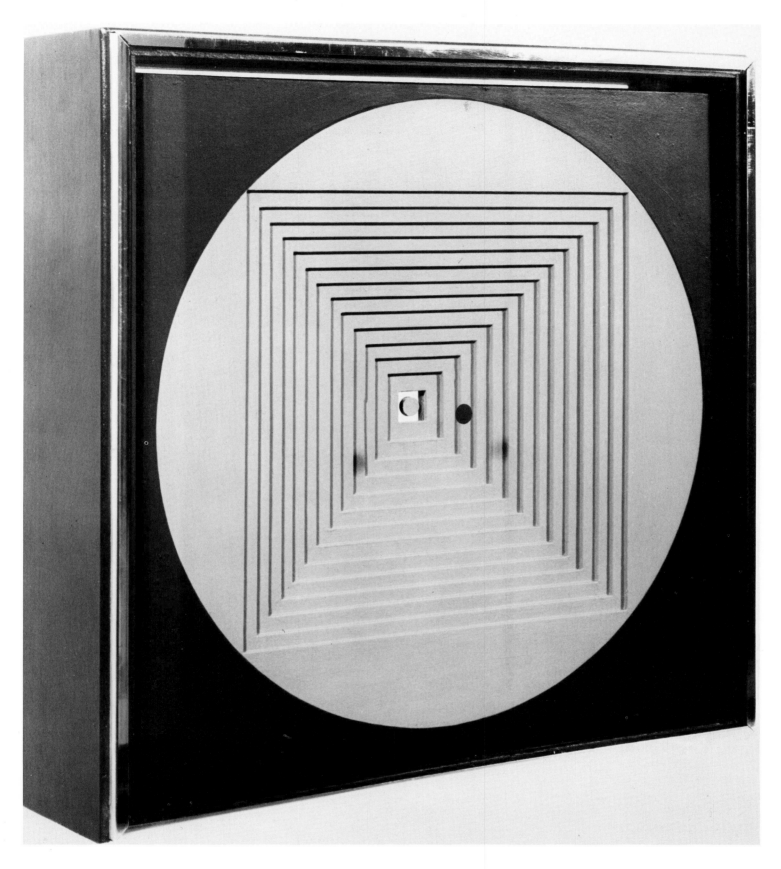

Mud Hut by Tony DeLap, 1968, glass, Plexiglas, stainless steel and paint, 15 x 15 x 4. Collection Whitney Museum of American Art, New York, gift of the Howard and Jean Lipman Foundation, Inc. Photo by Geoffrey Clements.

There is a great deal going on in the pattern within this box. Though the over-all construction is shallow, an illusion of perspective and depth is heightened by the placement of circles or dots that seem to give off shadows, which tends to make the box appear even deeper.

Tactile Tesseract by Ben Cunningham, construction for corner, 2 panels. Reproduced courtesy A. M. Sachs Gallery, New York. Photo by Djordje Milićević.

Scoring, fine lines and the clever placement of circles within squares achieve the effect of depth and inner dimension.

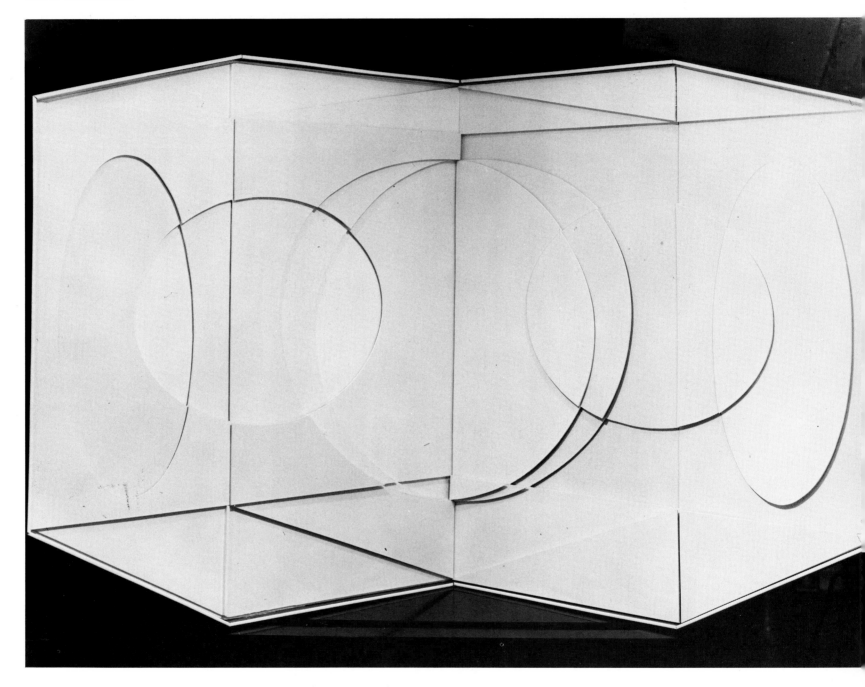

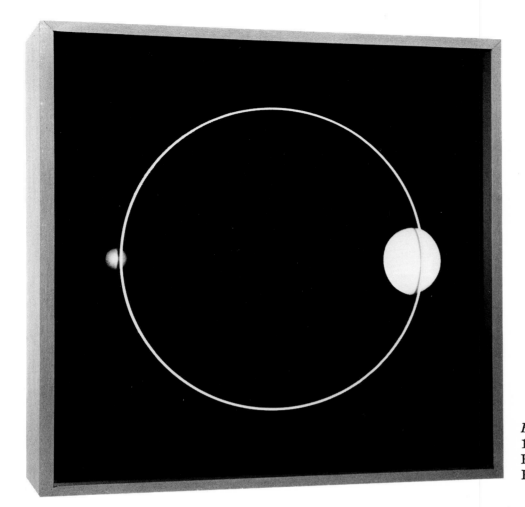

Binary No. 3 by John Willenbecher, 1965, construction, 17 x 17 x 5. Reproduced courtesy the artist. Photo by Geoffrey Clements.

Circles in boxes by Willenbecher

John Willenbecher's boxes are like telescopic views of the heavens. As if inspired by the space age, many of his compositions are celestial in theme and suggest geometric continuity to the infinite. Through the placement of his symbols, which always seem to be in a state of controlled motion, Willenbecher achieves the feeling of a very precise planetary order. His boxes portray both ideal beauty and elegance, and are almost like highly contemporary maps of the heavens.

Opposite page

Target with Four Faces by Jasper Johns, 1955, encaustic on newspaper, on canvas 26 x 25, surmounted by four plaster faces in a wooden frame 3¾ inches high. Collection The Museum of Modern Art, New York, gift of Mr. and Mrs. Robert C. Scull. Reproduced with kind permission.

Jasper Johns has remarked that a painting or a work of art consists of two elements: the artist's physical actions in creating it and the viewer's response or reaction in looking at it. In this work, concentric colored target rings were painted over the rough surface of a newsprint collage, while the four plaster-cast, identical but incomplete faces are contained in boxes above the target, their eyes shielded as if they were impassive observers (or are they the blind-folded condemned awaiting the firing squad?). There is a feeling of detachment about the faces, yet they relate to the visual excitement of the target.

Coca-Cola Plan by Robert Rauschenberg, 1958, collage, 68 x 64 x 12 cms. Collection Count Panza de Biumo, Milan. Reproduced with kind permission. Photo by Gian Sinigaglia.

Boxes by Jasper Johns, Rauschenberg, Oldenburg, Indiana, Trova, Mallory, Christo

Untitled Combine by Robert Rauschenberg, 1955, 220 x 94 x 67 cm. Collection Count Panza di Biumo, Milan. Reproduced with kind permission. Photo by Gian Sinigaglia.

"If you do not change your mind about something—when you confront a picture you have not seen before—you are either a stubborn fool or the painting is not very good."

Opposite page

Interview by Robert Rauschenberg, 1955, 185 x 125 cm. Collection Count Panza di Biumo, Milan. Reproduced with kind permission. Photo by Gian Sinigaglia.

Rauschenberg overflows or bursts the traditional dimensions of the canvas. "Painting," he wrote, "relates to both art and life. Neither can be made. I try to act in that gap between the two." His combine-pictures or collage paintings blend abstract brush work with ordinary found objects, cardboard, small boxes, clippings and photographs from periodicals and newspapers retaining both their individual identity and a strong presence. Rauschenberg maintains that ". . . paint itself is an object, and canvas, also. In my opinion, the void which must be filled, does not exist . . . I am trying to check my habits of seeing, to counter them for the sake of greater freshness. I am trying to be unfamiliar with what I am doing . . ."

Pastry Case II by Claes Oldenburg. Collection Mr. and Mrs. Morton G. Neumann. Photo by Eric Pollitzer. Reproduced with kind permission.

Exploding Numbers Box by Robert Indiana. Reproduced courtesy of the artist. Photo by Eric Pollitzer.

In one way or another, we see *Pastry Case* almost every day of our lives. Claes Oldenburg has enlarged its impact, thus enshrining it in our memories. Robert Indiana's *Exploding Numbers Box* is like a grouping of giant children's blocks. The beauty of the shape of the individual numbers makes an almost classical impression.

Mud-Muse by Robert Rauschenberg, driller's mud, sound and air-valve system, 48 x 108 x 144 feet. Collection Teledyne, Inc. Reproduced courtesy Los Angeles County Museum of Art, from the Art and Technology exhibition, 1971.

Mud-Muse is a 9 x 12 foot glass enclosure filled with brown mud which, when activated by a system of built-in air jets, bubbles at intermittent periods. The sound of the mud bubbles forming, bursting and re-forming is amplified by a series of strategically placed microphones and stereo speakers. The mud surface of the tank is in a state of almost constant change as it is activated by the air jets.

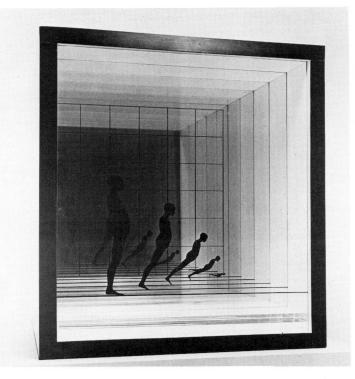

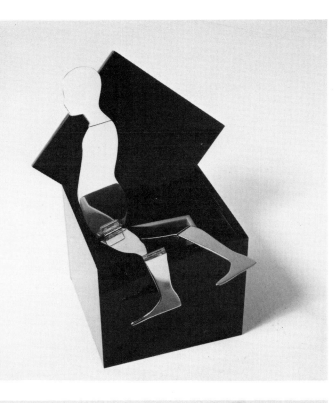

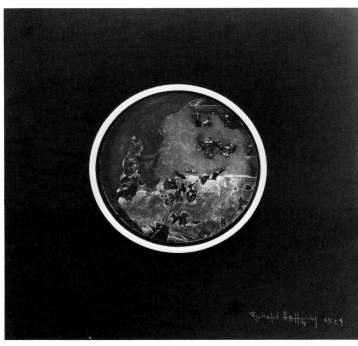

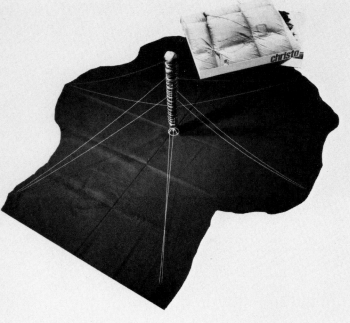

Above, left.
Study, Falling Man Series by **Ernest Trova**, 1964, plastic and mirror, 15½ x 13½ x 16⅞. Collection Howard W. Lipman, New York. Reproduced with kind permission.

Above, right.
Folding Man by **Ernest Trova**, 1968, hinged brass figure, 12 inches high, in black-and-red Plexiglas box, 5 x 5 x 5. Reproduced courtesy of Multiples Inc., New York.

Below, right.
Documenta Package by Christo, 1968, a box containing scale model of the Documenta IV monument, 3-dimensional storefront print, 2 signed and numbered color silkscreen and 7 black-and-white, signed-and-numbered prints, 24 x 24 x 6. Reproduced courtesy of Multiples Inc., New York.

Below, left.
Organa No. 6529 by Ronald Mallory, 1965, composition with mercury, Lucite frame and electric motor, 14½ x 14½. Collection, The Aldrich Museum, Ridgefield, Conn. Reproduced courtesy Dene Ulin, New York. Photo by Nathan Rabin.

Here are four good examples of the division of space within a box. In Trova's *Study, Falling Man Series*, the figure falls through a system of grids to a diminishing point. In his *Folding Man*, a cube takes on its own spatial characteristics. (See also pages 214 and 215.) In *Organa No. 6529*, Ronald Mallory achieves depth for his box through target-like placement of the circular window. In *Documenta Package*, Christo's parachute-like package appears to be floating in space, despite the strong suggestion that it is tied down or anchored to land.

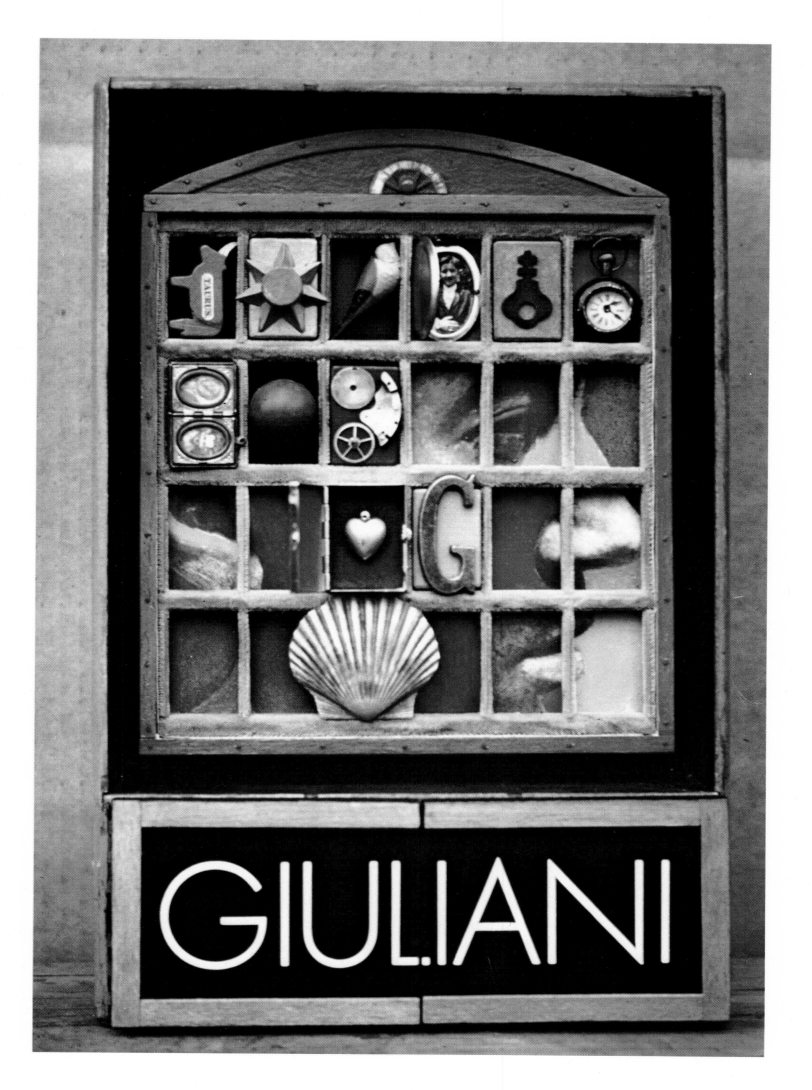

Vin Giuliani's boxes have style and stamina. Fanciful, imaginative, elegant icons in spirit, they cleverly portray 20th-century vignettes in a step-by-step, block-by-block manner reminiscent of the Renaissance.

Giuliani's images are composed of softly colored blocks and pieces of wood fashioned to fit together as carefully as mosaic tesserae. Small nails are used to hold the composition together, their placement serving to coordinate and unite the multi-colored, multi-shaped pieces into a unique harmony. He also incorporates both found and dime-store objects, as well as small mirrors, into his work with the same precision. The geometry of his work, and the occasional mysterious symbolism, always produce a sense of movement and an unusual feeling of delight. Somehow Giuliani succeeds in fascinating with a child-like but far from childish approach; only upon introspection do you realize the grandeur of his sophistication.

Box by Vin Giuliani. Reproduced courtesy of the artist.

Opposite page

A series of boxes by Vin Giuliani. Reproduced, as is the box on page 157, courtesy of the artist.

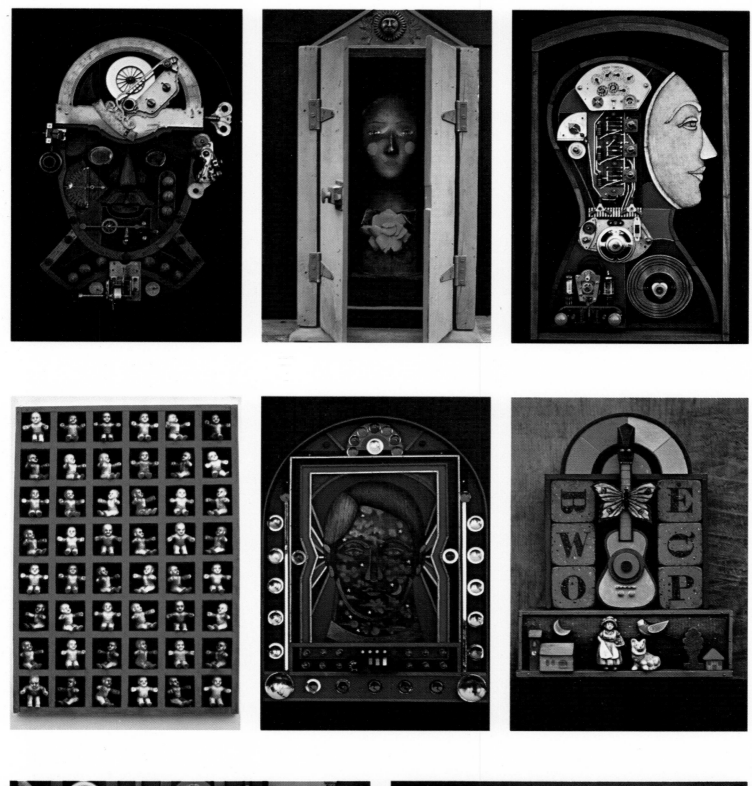

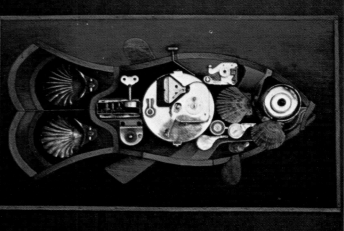

Untitled Box No. 3 by Lucas
Samaras, 1963, wood, pins, rope,
and stuffed bird, 24½ x 11½ x 10¼.
Collection Whitney Museum of
American Art, New York, gift of
the Howard and Jean Lipman
Foundation, Inc. Photo by Geoffrey
Clements. Reproduced with kind
permission.

The box is ecological in appearance,
nest-like. One would not want to
intrude on its inhabitant. There's
something both tender and private
inside. The falling twine or rope is
fascinating; it is something which
might be gathered for a nest but
not for this nest, which appears to
be built to precise dimensions,
as if by a machine.

160

Samaras

Lucas Samaras has been quoted as saying, "I find high erotic content in things iridescent, sparkling, fragile, sharp, oily, hairy, pimply, fluffy, dendritic, elastic, pulsating. I love mirrors, shadows, vortexes, lightning, razzle-dazzle, twistedness and nausea, but all these things with control."

A leading exponent of working with the tactile qualities of urban waste, of using whatever material comes to hand, Samaras first made boxes constructed of colored plastic sheeting and numerous pieces of mirror; the intention was to reflect the aspects of the environment in which the box was created and placed.

Samaras once exhibited a unique box—an actual life-size room of mirrors with furniture constructed of mirrors as well. Upon entering, the viewer was assaulted with a series of multiple self-images. It was, in a way, what Samaras had done in earlier years by incorporating everyday objects into his compositions, so that recognizable forms could be seen in a new context. This time the familiar form being thrust into a new environment was the viewer himself.

Chicken Wire Box No. 16 by Lucas Samaras, 1972, acrylic paint on chicken wire, 18 x 12½ x 16. Collection Mr. and Mrs. Joel Ehrenkranz, New York. Reproduced courtesy Pace Gallery, New York. Photo by Al Mozell.

Stiff Box No. 5 by Lucas Samaras, 1971, steel, 12¾ x 16 x 8. Reproduced courtesy Pace Gallery, New York.

Right. Box No. 55 by Lucas Samaras, 1966, mixed media, 12½ x 16 x 12. Collection Eugene Schwartz. Reproduced courtesy Pace Gallery, New York.

Below. Childhood by Don Shaw. Reproduced courtesy Dianne David, Houston.

Though Don Shaw's *Childhood* is almost like an abstract textural painting there are some very recognizable objects in it—four playing-card games at the extremities of the composition, a woman's shoe and a childhood photograph. There is a sense of time to what we see, as the title suggests.

Phoenix by Alfonso Ossorio, 1968, 72 x 60. Reproduced courtesy Cordier & Ekstrom, Inc., New York. Photo by Geoffrey Clements.

The intermingling and interlocking of a multitude of objects and items produce a textural, futuristic composition.

Textures

The artist can succeed in disguising the original box by his use of textures on the inner surfaces or by placing textured objects inside. The box, on the other hand, performs its function, that of creating a new awareness of the treatment of surfaces.

Some of the boxes in this section use painterly techniques to good advantage, mixing illusions of depth on flat surfaces and illusions of flatness on three-dimensional areas so that finally the whole becomes a play of textures. The Gregory Gillespie box (see page 165) is quiet, restful, even delicate, and has a point of perspective leading the viewer into a poetic countryside scene. The surrounding textures are organized and controlled, telescoping towards the principal image within the composition. Arthur Secunda's *The Artist As A Young Man* (see page 166) has as many objects in it as the Gillespie composition, but the treatment is vastly different. His box has no center and no edges. The objects, varying in size and quality, are highly disorganized. More than anything else the viewer is aware of textures.

In these compositions, as well as others depicted, the box, because of the artist's use of texture, takes on all the attributes and characteristics of a vibrant abstract painting.

Assemblage No. 6 by Susan Brown (8 panels), 1966. Reproduced courtesy of the artist.

Susan Brown believes that "...ideas are compelling...persisting until a response is evoked."

"This inexplicable creative process," she continues, "is the basic motivation for my existence.

Whether I'm exploring the potential of wood, stone, clay, synthetics, found objects or fibers...or whether I'm using appliqué, assemblage, crochet, embroidery or stuffed forms as my technique, the excitement experienced in working is my reward. When someone else likes the result of my work, that's a bonus."

Exterior Wall with Landscape by Gregory Gillespie, 1967, mixed media, 38¼ x 23¾ x 4. Reproduced courtesy The Hirshhorn Museum and Sculpture Garden, Smithsonian Institution, Washington, D.C.

This wall, looking like something out of the Renaissance with its layer upon layer of seemingly accumulated depth, has a *trompe l'oeil* quality about it. The mixture of flat painted surfaces and of dimension is most subtle. The eye cannot determine where one begins and the other ends. The figures journey in and out of the wall almost at random, and the viewer can't really decide if they are resting on its surfaces, embedded in it or coming through it from some mysterious place on the other side. The composition, with what seems an entire civilization compressed in it, is a time-capsule in the form of a box.

Top left.
Untitled by Jane Evans, 1972, construction of painted wood, 96 x 108. Reproduced courtesy The Aldrich Museum, Ridgefield, Conn.

Top right.
Small Mountain in a Box by Ira Joel Haber, 1971, mixed media, 6⅝ x 2⅛ x 5¼. Collection Lawrence Di Carlo and A. Alador Marberger. Reproduced courtesy Fischbach Gallery, New York.

Bottom left.
The Artist as a Young Man by Arthur Secunda, 1972, polyester assemblage, 19½ x 14 x 1⅝. Reproduced courtesy The Aldrich Museum, Ridgefield, Conn.

Bottom right.
Mushrooms and Toast by Sari Dienes, 1965, 18 x 9 x 1½. Reproduced courtesy Phenix, New York.

Most of the objects and forms in these four boxes are very personal to the artists concerned. The mixtures and intermingling within each create their own textures and imagery. The viewer is aware of wood and dripping paint intermingling, clouds and rocks being contrasted with each other, the contemporary and the old being thrown together pell-mell. Both surrealism and aspects of decay seem to be part of the overall feeling projected in one way or another in all of these box compositions.

Untitled (from the series *Industrial Petrification*) by Luis Perelman, 1964, polyester resin and mixed media, 12½ x 9¼ x 4½. Collection Whitney Museum of American Art, New York, gift of the Howard and Jean Lipman Foundation, Inc. Photo by Geoffrey Clements. Reproduced with kind permission.

Again the viewer is conscious of objects being thrown together almost at random. How and where they have fallen has created accidental pattern and texture. Unlike the boxes on the opposite page, the artist has frozen his composition in transparent plastic, enabling the viewer to see the objects from all sides, as if the box were a piece of sculpture.

167

Right. 80 rectangles sur 20 plans inclinés (80 rectangles on 20 inclined planes) by Pol Bury, 1964, 110 x 50 x 24 cm. Collection Mr. and Mrs. P. Silverman, Toronto. Photo courtesy Lefebre Gallery, New York, taken by André Morain. Reproduced with kind permission.

Center. 7 Boules, 5 Cubes (7 balls, 5 cubes) by Pol Bury, wood and mechanism. Reproduced courtesy the J. L. Hudson Gallery, Detroit.

Below. 3 Cubes by Pol Bury, 1968, stainless steel, 47 x 15¾ x 15¾. Reproduced courtesy Moos Gallery, Ltd., Toronto.

29 Lattes Verticales (29 Vertical Laths) by Pol Bury, wood and mechanism. Reproduced courtesy The J. L. Hudson Gallery, Detroit.

Pol Bury

Pol Bury's box sculptures and constructions convey anticipation— as if you were awaiting the arrival of a storm. Something will happen but you don't quite know what! Though the elements within his boxes, guided by motorized magnets, move slowly, the effect on the viewer is far less gradual: dreams, inner reflections, hallucinations, sensuous appeal, fascination....

Bury's shapes consist of highly polished steel or metal cubes and columns, spheres and circular objects usually in normal or regular size. The motion of the elements is hardly noticeable. What is created is a feeling of the infinite, of time and of space. The movement is organized, almost preordained, like the earth journeying from day to night and then to day again. The impact, many times heightened by the magnificent reflections on the sides, the top and the floor of the box, is enormous.

64 Balls Reflecting (detail) by Pol
Bury, 1968, copper, 31½ x 31½ x 8.
Reproduced courtesy Moos Gallery,
Ltd., Toronto.

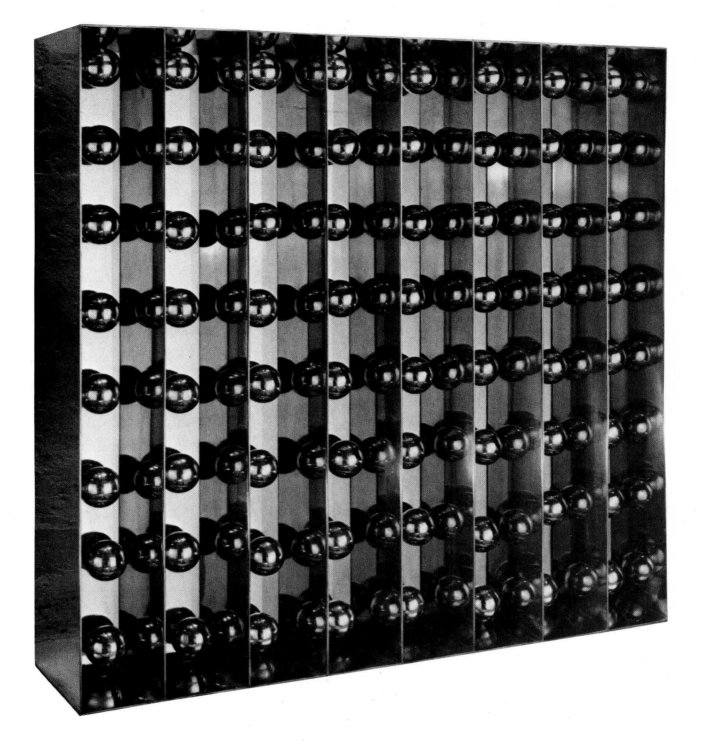

Box constructions by Pol Bury.
Reproduced courtesy Galerie Maeght,
Paris.

Decorated Look-In Machine by Norman Laliberté.

The box is fascinating to look at from the outside. The fact that it houses a show of some kind appears to be of secondary interest. Painted and incised wood cut-outs have been affixed to the sides of the box to carry out the show or theater motif.

Box enclosure for the bar area at
La Fonda del Sol. The box containing the circus-like figures was set
into an 18-inch thick wall, and
was visible from both sides. A second
view is seen below.

Boxes by Girard

Photographs by Charles and Ray Eames

The child will treasure a favorite toy or doll long after he or she has ceased playing with it, for it symbolizes a specific time and place in that young person's unique history. Similarly, folk-art collections of dolls and toy objects represent the way a nation or a people identify themselves with the past, and serve to recall a lifestyle rapidly vanishing or now long since gone.

Alexander Girard, one of America's foremost designers and architects, more than two decades ago created the Girard Foundation as a depository for the folk dolls and remarkable toy objects he has collected from many parts of the world.

The folk art of Latin America (Mexico, Peru, Ecuador, Guatemala, Bolivia, Brazil and Costa Rica) was the source of one of Alexander Girard's best known design projects—the La Fonda del Sol Restaurant in New York (1960 to 1970), where the walls were inset with dozens of look-in boxes, each portraying a scene or vignette from Latin American life through an arrangement of original dolls and toys from the period portrayed.

Speaking of the figures within these unusual boxes, Mr. Girard has written: "Today these toys... communicate to us the powerful spirit of an unusual and highly imaginative people. For the most part they are the expression of a naive and unsophisticated people who have lived close to the earth... The objects communicate directness, simplicity and firm spiritual beliefs... as well as humor, whimsy, tragedy and love... Wisdom and gratitude demand that we acknowledge their message... appealing to the children within us... we are invited to translate their meaning into terms of our own experience..."

The boxes at La Fonda del Sol were photographed by Charles and Ray Eames and reproduced with their cooperation and the permission of Alexander Girard.

Above. Part of a recess with a collection of magic or voodoo figures and dolls from Bahia, Brazil, made of wood, iron and pottery and representing devils and fertility figures.

Page 176

Above. The area at the top of this photograph (lace effect) depicts a box in the dining area showing a group of figures from Tehuantepéc, Mexico. The bottom or principal part of this photo depicts a market place with four large painted pottery figures from Ocotlán, Mexico. In front of these is an assembly of containers filled with market produce ... some real (beans) others artificial (fruit and vegetables).

Below. A series of boxes in the La Fonda del Sol bar enclosure. At top, center, a sun designed by Alexander Girard in Lima, Peru, and made by native craftsmen; at its right, a plaster church from Mexico; and to the right of that, a painted pottery church from Metepéc, Mexico. Also seen are boxes containing the three kings on horse, camel and elephant, from Cuzco, Peru; a miniature kitchen from Puebla, Mexico; a papier mâché devil from Celaya, Mexico; a painted wood chest from Olinala, Mexico; a pottery church from Ayacucho, Peru; and artificial flowers from various Latin American countries.

Poppet Gom Theatre Scarabee, box containing text, musical scores, themes and sets of theater pieces, from Antwerp, Holland. Reproduced courtesy Archive Jean Brown, The Shaker Seed House, Tyringham, Mass.

A-Z detail of "a contributive picture," by Joe Tilson, 1963, mixed media on wood relief, 92 x 60. Reproduced courtesy Marlborough Fine Arts (London) Ltd.

Numbers, letters and words combine to give dynamic quality to the *Poppet Gom Theatre Scarabee* box. It makes a strong poster-like statement about its very presence and state of being. The letters in Tilson's *A-Z* composition are three dimensional; each has been placed in its own compartment to create additional emphasis through isolation. The figures, forms and photographs above each letter—P for popsicle or Q for question mark, for instance—are like the artist's personal visual alphabet.

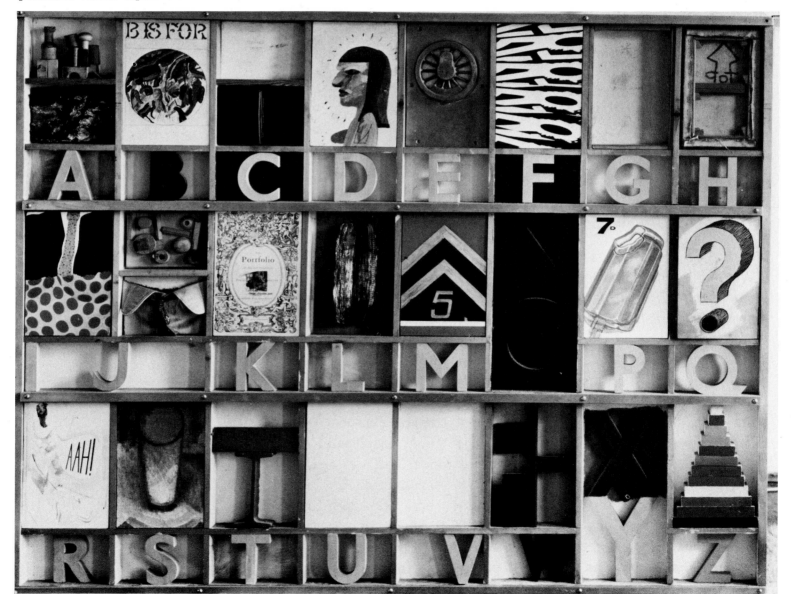

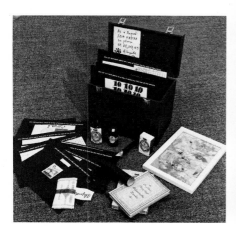

Fluxus Year Box 2, 1968, containing works by George Brecht, Ben Vautier, Bob Watts, Yoko Ono, Willem de Ridder, Paul Sharits, Albert Fine, F. Lieberman and Sohei Hashimoto. Reproduced courtesy Archive Jean Brown, The Shaker Seed House, Tyringham, Mass.

Box containing exhibition catalogues of the Paolo Soleri Retrospective at the Corcoran Art Gallery, Washington, D.C., 1970. Reproduced courtesy Archive Jean Brown, The Shaker Seed House, Tyringham, Mass.

Unknown Game No. 3 by John Willenbecher, 1963, 27½ x 18 x 4. Reproduced courtesy of the artist. Photo by Oliver Baker.

Continue by Arthur Köpcke. Reproduced courtesy Galerie René Block, Berlin. Photo by Hilde Zenker.

In *Fluxus Year Box 2,* black and red stenciled letters and figures on bare wood serve as a title page to the contents of the box. A printed paper tightly wrapped and glued around a box container serves the same function for the Paolo Soleri catalogues. Letters and numbers in different type faces combine to form vital elements in *Unknown Game,* and in *Continue* we have a combination of printed objects—rolls, flat sheets, smaller boxes, bottles, dividers—all of which use letters and numbers that are hand-printed or applied with press-on or photostat materials. *Obelisk,* a tall and elongated pyramid, would be fairly monotonous standing by itself, but by inserting numbers from zero to one, the box takes on or creates its own particular sense of drama. It is a calendar, a clock or even a visual countdown for a rocket about to be launched. Without the numbers in that particular position and composition, the obelisk would be quite ordinary.

1234567890 Obelisk by Joe Tilson, 1963, painted wood, 40½ inches high. Reproduced courtesy Marlborough Fine Arts (London) Ltd.

The Kiosk by Sidney Simon, 1960, polychromed maple and birch, 37 x 24. Reproduced courtesy of the artist.

The composition represents the artist's humorous interpretation of a newspaper seller, part of Simon's *Hero* series depicting individuals without whom everyday life would be altered considerably. Simon has built the newspaper stand and its occupant through the use of old type faces and blocks of type. The newspaper has become the vendor, the vendor the newspaper and the over-all composition a powerful symbol of the press medium.

Opposite page

The Voyeur by David McManaway, 1972, mixed media, 13½ x 10½. Photo courtesy Paul Rogers Harris, Dallas, taken by Hickey and Robertson. Reproduced courtesy of the artist.

The three distinct objects, each in their own section, make for a most eloquent box. The word "love" inside its own box, standing on a pedestal surrounded by fur, and the rose, all by itself in a delicate vase, seem to define one another. The object opposite the flower is unusual; on wheels as if ready to flee and peering over the little wall, it seems to convey the message of the title of the composition.

180

Construction No. 84, by Leroy Lamis,
1965, Plexiglas, 24 x 12. Reproduced
courtesy Staempfli Gallery, New
York and The Aldrich Museum,
Ridgefield, Conn. Photo by John D.
Schiff.

A series of transparent plastic boxes,
one inside the other, seem to lead
towards infinity.

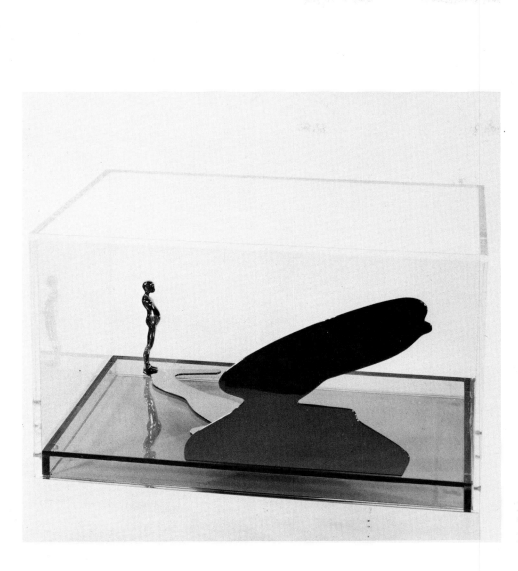

Plexiglas Box Construction by Ernest Trova. Reproduced courtesy Galerie Moos, Inc., Montreal.

Transparent and Translucent Boxes

The transparent and translucent boxes that follow are almost complete opposites to the hinged and pull-drawer boxes depicted earlier. Now the box compositions are completely open and revealing, and, if there are secrets, they center around artistic meaning rather than what shape or form may be hidden within the box. A transparent box contains but it does not conceal, and this gives the artist still another dimension with which to cope.

Transparent and translucent boxes are of new materials, plastic and Plexiglas being the most predominant. Color, either injected into the plastic when it was being formed or applied in the traditional way, plays an important role in these compositions, as does natural or artificial lighting. Here, too, objects play a great part as well as the use of multiples, mirrors, and natural materials. The environment in which the box is set assumes greater importance than before, as it can be seen through as well as around the box composition itself.

Stacked No. 1 by Ida Kohlmeyer, 1969, 31 x 9 x 9. Reproduced courtesy of the artist. Photo by Stuart Lynn.

"These painted constructions represent the only sustained excursion I have made into the third dimension. At the time, I felt compelled to make 'objects,' and being fundamentally a painter, I leaned very heavily on old habits which, naturally, focused on painted surfaces. Actually, I used the same material to paint on that I did for easel paintings. They were built of wood, canvas covered and usually encased in Plexiglas, the latter both for protection and a more spatial effect . . .

"The new thing about the constructions, for me, was their 'thinginess.' I could embrace them. They seemed less illusory than paintings. Space surrounded them, and I was relieved from having to induce it . . ."

Opposite page

Top row: Chair No. 1, 1969, oil wood, Plexiglas and canvas; *Pyramidal No. 1* (side 2), 1969; *Quinary 9″ Cube No. 3*, 1969, oil, wood, Plexiglas and canvas.

Second row: Quinque No. 1 (side 2), 1969; *Stacked No. 1*, 1969; *Quarto No. 1*, 1969.

Third row: Quinary 9″ Cube No. 4, 1969; *Quinary 9″ Cube No. 4* (side 2), 1969, *Quarto No. 1*, (side 2), 1969.

Bottom row: 3D Circlet No. 4 (side 2), 1969; *3D Circlet No. 4* (side 1), 1969; *Quadruped No. 3* (side 2).

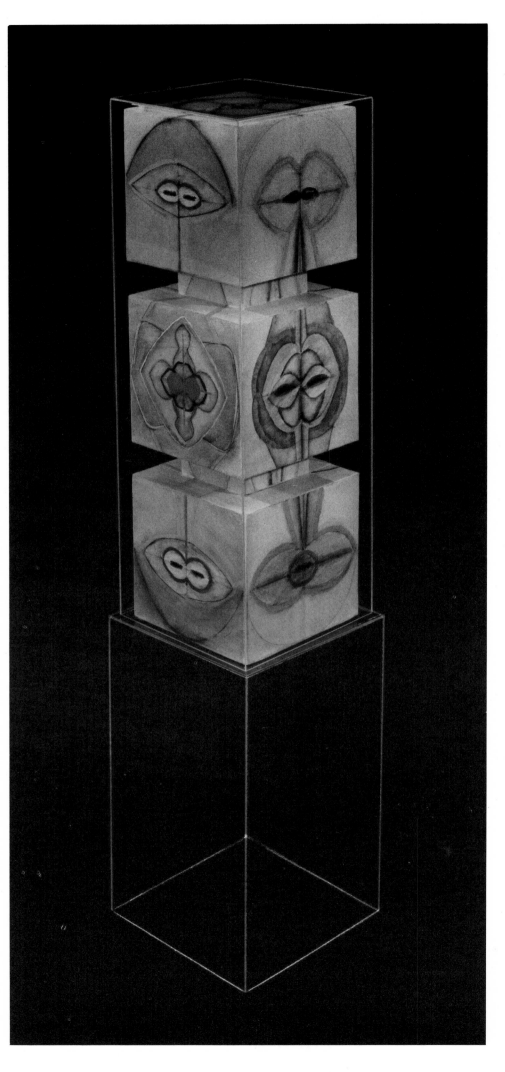

184

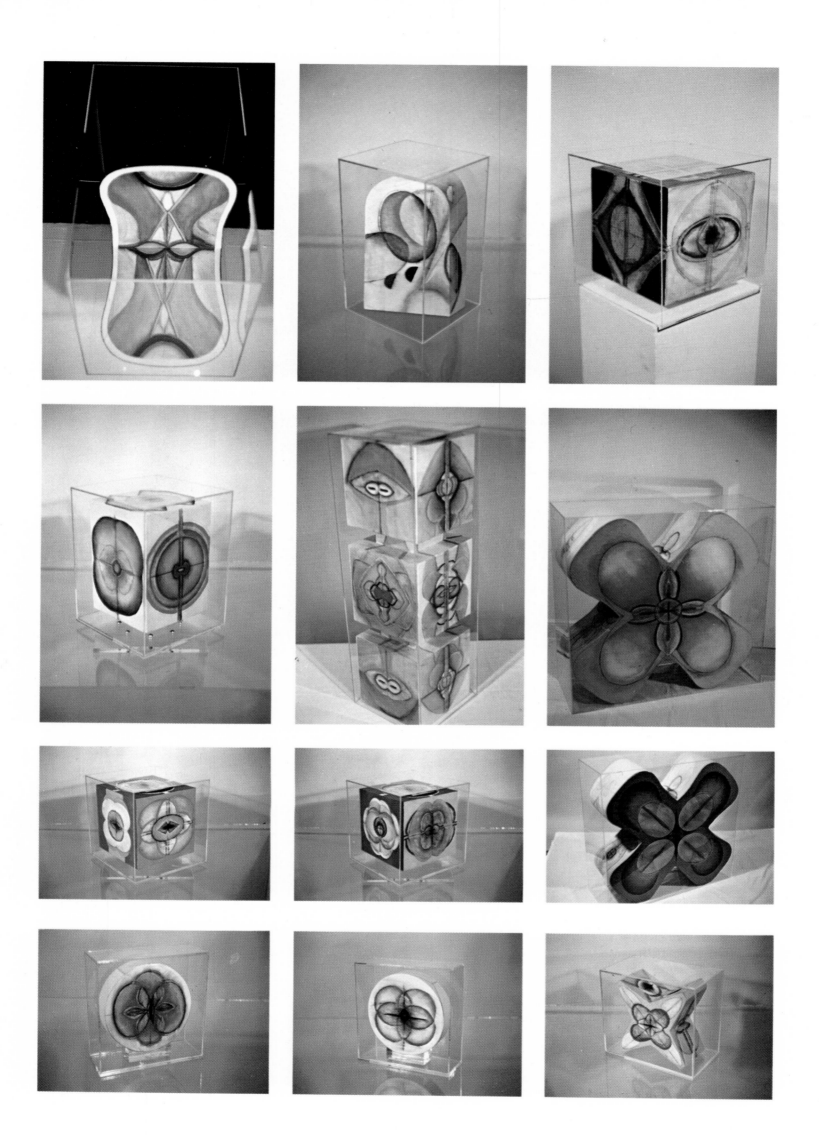

Home or Reflections on the Interior by Robert Naess, 1972, construction of mold-blown, free-formed glass and sheet glass. Collection Robert L. Pfannebecker. Reproduced courtesy of the artist.

The composition consists of interior glass shelving within a glass house with gold glass molded human objects such as brains and fetuses, while a series of mirrors serves as the windows of the structure. At first view, it looks like a Greek temple, a shimmering cathedral or a fabled ice-palace of czarist days. One also gets the impression of looking into and through a transparent figure or body.

". . . The objects themselves and their relationship to a work are crystallizations of images and symbols emotionally and physically habitual in my living during a given stretch of time. I came to hot glass, or blown glass, by way of using other materials, and once I started playing with molten glass, I stayed to learn the techniques unique to its use. Materials are like a varied diet which I explore over a long period of time, using different kinds of materials for new explorations."

Opposite Page

The boxes illustrated are all made of transparent materials and, for the most part, have transparent surfaces, although some have been painted to make them opaque and others have been tinted to give special effects to the lighting. In addition, some of these constructions rely on a play of various translucencies, achieved by tinting or by thick pieces of plastic, and others on subdivision by panels and cubes. In one or two instances, color defines walls or highlights specific sections of the interior.

Top and bottom. Four and Five Squares by Françoise Sullivan, 1965, transparent acrylic. Reproduced courtesy Dorothy Cameron, Toronto. Photo by John Reeves.

Left, above. Island by Derek Michael Besant.

Left, below. Box by Françoise Sullivan, 1968. Photo courtesy Dorothy Cameron, Toronto.

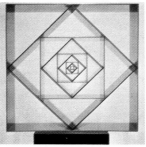

Right, above. Untitled by Robert Naess.

Right, below. Cents Sign by Chryssa, 1969, Plexiglas, steel and enamel paint.

Magiscope by Feliciano Bejar. Reproduced courtesy The New Bertha Schaefer Gallery, Inc., New York.

Untitled by Larry Bell, 1969, coated glass and metal 12⅛ x 12⅛ x 12⅛. Reproduced courtesy of the artist. Photo by Frank J. Thomas.

These boxes, and those on the opposite page, are similar in initial appearance but vastly different in the way the effects are achieved. In Bejar's *Magiscope,* a series of lenses captures light, atmosphere and environment, distorting these in concave and convex reflection (see page 201 for a closer view). Bell's composition is a contemplative box; because it is empty the viewer projects his thoughts into it. Thomson's *Equivocations,* on the other hand, is a grid within a grid, a visually filled composition. The components can be arranged, stacked or nestled in numerous ways (see page 190 for another view). Bell's box is even more dynamic through the clever use of bands of paint set on reflective surfaces, which creates a whirling effect within the limitation of its own space; this serves to enlarge the inside space of the box optically, far in excess of its actual proportions.

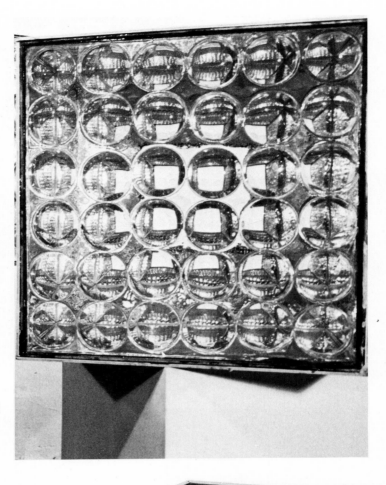

Equivocations by Betty Thomson, acrylic, 50 x 50 x 50 cm. Reproduced courtesy Alecto International, London and New York.

Untitled by Larry Bell, 1965, glass and chrome, 14¼ x 14¼. Reproduced courtesy of The Aldrich Museum, Ridgefield, Conn. Photo by Howard Harrison.

The Swiss Pavilion at Expo '70, Osaka, Japan. Reproduced courtesy Trade Fairs and Special Events Office, Suisse d'expansion commerciale, Zurich.

Glass, transparent and translucent materials, anodized aluminum, and the use of light in box and multiple box structures were central to the design concept of the Pavilion of Switzerland at Expo '70, Osaka, Japan.

Named a "Radiant Structure" by its planners, and a "Tree of Light" by thousands of visitors, the exterior of the Swiss Pavilion resembled a neat pile of light boxes suspended in mid-air, so to speak, and almost floating over the artificial body of water it fronted. A suspended ceiling composed of a multitude of lights recessed in what resembled a series of multiple boxes, dominated the interior. Display cases were columnar, appearing like seven transparent boxes precisely piled from floor to ceiling. The square construction of the outside patio or terrace and of the interior flooring heightened the Pavilion's overall box-like qualities, which can be seen in the view on page 61.

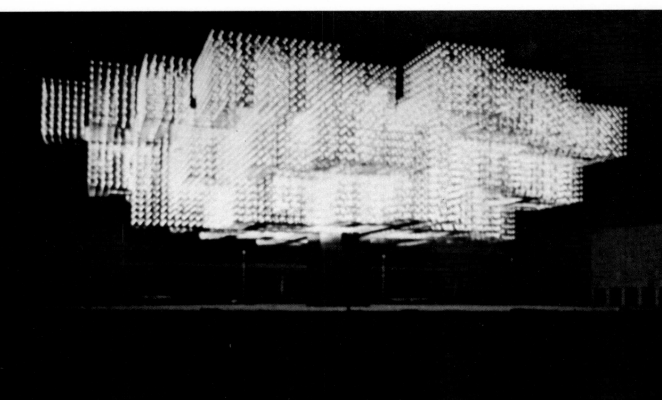

Magiscope by Feliciano Bejar. Reproduced courtesy The New Bertha Schaefer Gallery, Inc., New York.

Feliciano Bejar, who has worked in wood, stone and metal, commenced experimentation with glass in the early 1960s, and developed techniques in crystal, plastic and metal, as well as refinements in grinding lenses, tempering plastic and polishing metal, all of which he uses to great advantage in his constructions and boxes, which he calls Magiscopes (see page 198).

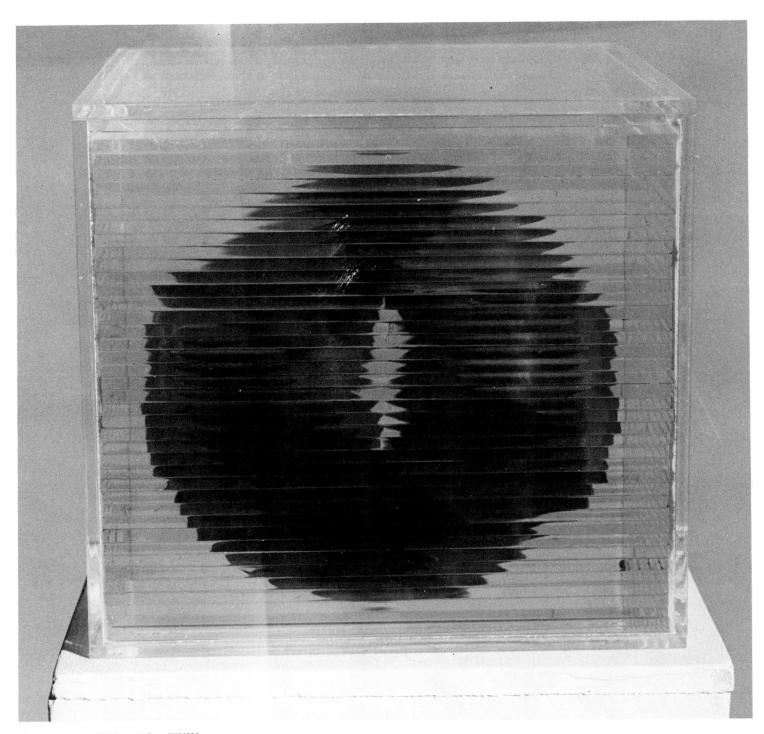

Réfraction IV by John William
Lavender, 1968, Plexiglas and silk-
screen, 10½ x 10½ x 10½. Collection
Musée d'Art Contemporain,
Montreal. Reproduction with kind
permission.

Lavender and Zammitt (whose
work is on the opposite page)
use almost identical methods of
breaking up space within a confined
area, but evoke different sensations
of movement (or lack of it).
Lavender encloses his shape by using
strips to form a broken down circle,
not unlike an object frozen in ice.
Zammitt employs multi-level
transparent panels, which transmit
light so that different shades and
shadows come into being, suggesting
a condition of continuous change.

202

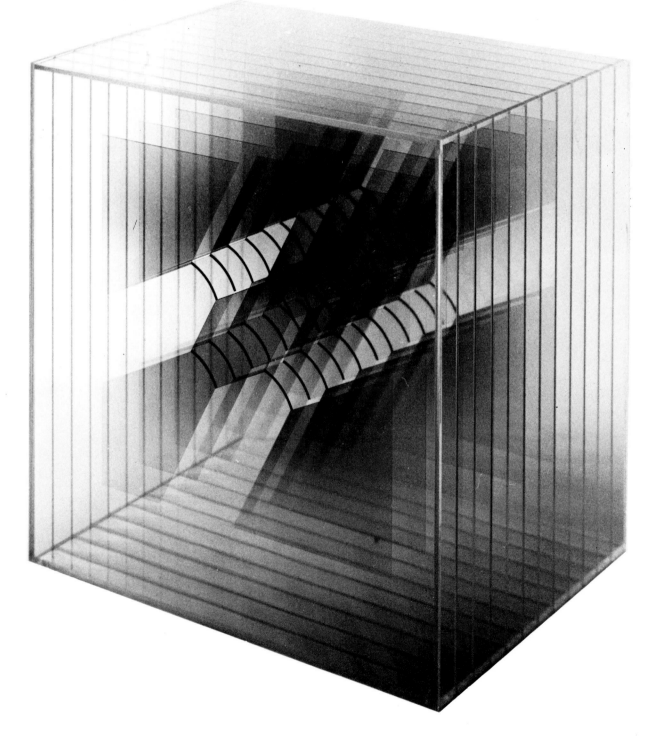

Untitled by Norman Zammitt, 1965,
construction, baked enamel on acrylic
plastic. Collection Stephen Booke,
Los Angeles. Reproduced courtesy
of the artist.

Condensation Cage by Hans Haacke, 1963/65, acrylic, water and climate of environment. Reproduced courtesy of the artist. Photo by the artist.

The artist's task according to Hans Haacke, is to ". . . make something which experiences, reacts to its environment, changes, is non-stable . . .

". . . make something indeterminate, which always looks different, the shape of which cannot be predicted precisely . . .

". . . make something which cannot 'perform' without the assistance of its environment . . .

". . . make something which reacts to light and temperature changes, is subject to air currents and depends, in its functioning, on the forces of gravity . . .

". . . make something which the 'spectator' handles, with which he plays, and thus animates . . .

". . . make something which lives in time and makes the 'spectator' experience time . . .

". . . articulate something natural . . ."

Rainbox by Hans Haacke, 1963, acrylic and water. Reproduced courtesy of the artist. Photo by the artist.

Air, steam, water, ice—all of which have invisible attributes that enable them to transform into one another—are the major forces at work in this box structure of Hans Haacke, which is reversed for activation. His works embrace a basic philosophy: ". . . the world . . . is something dynamic, something that constantly changes, something that is always on the move, never permitting a status quo . . ."

While most art seeks physical permanence, Hans Haacke's boxes concern motion and almost constant regeneration. Contained in see-through Plexiglas boxes, the reaction of one element on the other (for example water going through the process of condensation) forms the composition, and explores the effect of gravity and the other forces which induce condensation, freezing, or misting.

Haacke seeks to demonstrate that the illusion of change is not an illusion at all, but real; change is constant. The contents of his boxes react to their environment and are never stationary. The responsive systems of nature will never produce exactly the same visual result the next day, or for that matter, the same afternoon. The viewer must deal with what results (almost for him alone) at the particular instant that he is seeing the work.

Single Dropper by Hans Haacke,
1963, acrylic and water. Reproduced
courtesy of the artist. Photo by
the artist.

This box is also reversed to set it in
motion.

"The working premise is to think
in terms of systems; the production
of systems, the interference with
and the exposure of existing systems.

"Such an approach is concerned
with the operational structure of
organizations, in which transfer of
information, energy and/or material
occurs. Systems can be physical,
biological or social; they can be
man-made, naturally existing or a
combination of any of the above."

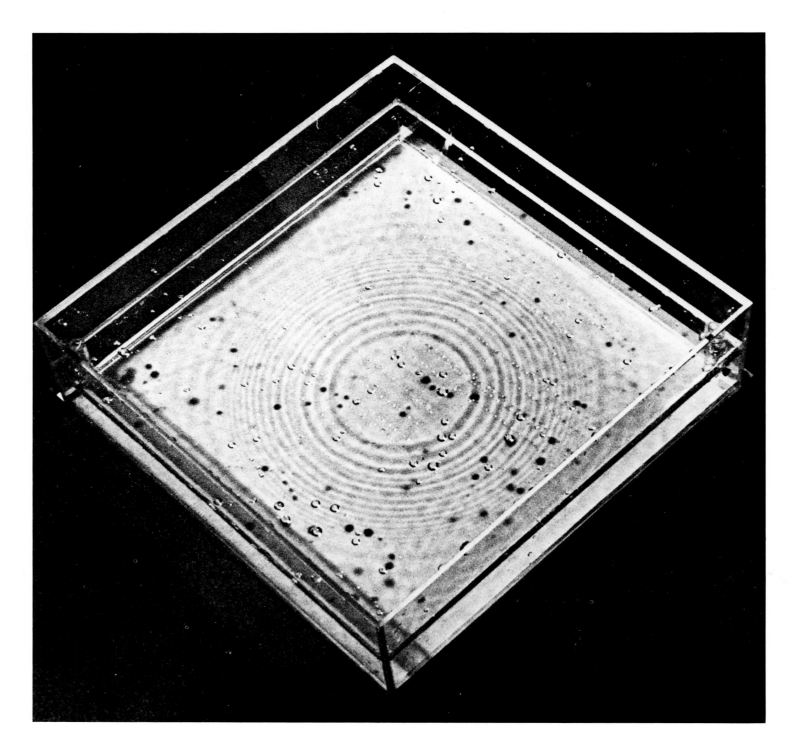

A display in Man the Producer, one
of the theme buildings at Expo '67,
Montreal. Acrylic cubes, in this
instance representing and containing
the elements of a tree, formed an
integral part of an exhibition
delineating the importance of earth,
sea and atmosphere to all that
mankind does. Transparent and
translucent boxes played a dominant
part in the form and design of
all parts of the exhibition.

Plateaus by Aaronel deRoy Gruber, clear acrylic boxes enclosing a series of progressions of colored vacuum-formed plastic squares, with mirror backing and lighting. Reproduced courtesy of the artist. Photographs by Walt Seng.

"Technical construction, while interesting, detailed and strenuous, should not be a consideration of the viewer. The viewer should be involved with aesthetics. I sometimes use movement—spinning by hand or motors, or reverse motions— things to involve the viewer.

"Art to me is vision, to reveal and contemplate our insight or inner sight through contemplation. Art is not an object, but an experience. To perceive or be moved, one needs to be receptive.

"I want to achieve a variety in sameness with the variety through series progressions, color placement, lighting or movement.

"I want the sculptures to be pristine, to eliminate most excesses, yet not to be empty; to form a kaleidoscope view for the observer.

"Artists are to create, not explain . . ."

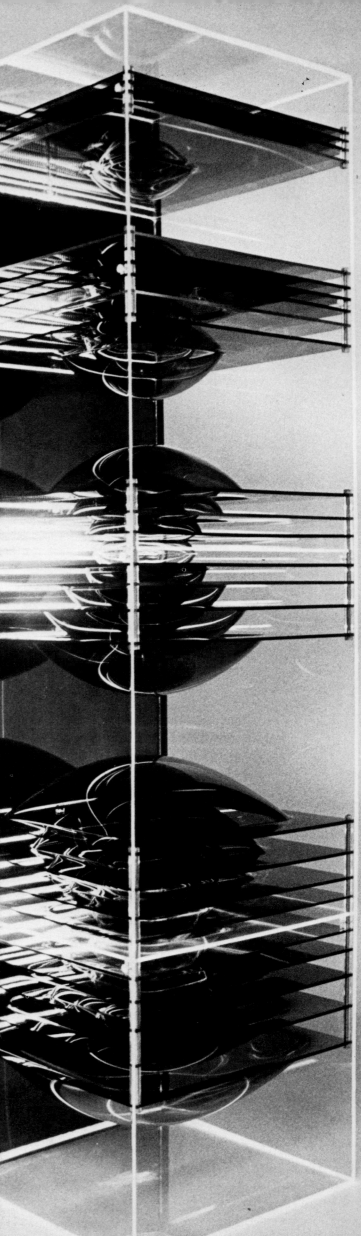

208

Three Plus One by Aaronel deRoy Gruber, 1968, clear Plexiglas, 54 x 24. Reproduced courtesy of the artist. Photo by Jacob Malezi.

"My most recent work is involved with pyramid and oval shapes and continuing the rounded square in three-dimensional form, using transparent vacuum-formed constructions. In developing a forward and backward visual thrust, the constructions project in and out within a cube, rectangle or obelisk. The varied views produce myriad images created by light, reflections and shadows, expanding classic geometric forms without symbolic references.

"Who can say that words are actually communicative or that conveying one's thoughts can express the message we intend? The vision that produces the message comes from a vast number of ideas so individual and so private as to be almost solipsistic. Self is the only object of verifiable knowledge."

December, 1969, University of Calgary, Alberta (detail) by Glenn Lewis, 4 pieces of mirror Plexiglas, burnt paper originally 100 yards by 100 yards square. Reproduced courtesy The Douglas Gallery, Vancouver.

The box and burnt paper somehow present the calm of accepted destiny. Whatever was destroyed had to be destroyed. The unknown terror is over, and this is the proof of it.

Box L by Lucas Samaras, 1964,
mixed media, 17 x 25⅛ x 11¼.
Reproduced courtesy The Aldrich
Museum, Ridgefield, Conn.
Photo by Walter J. Russell.

The artist has encased a great many
transparent materials in a clear
plastic box. The objects seem placed
at random and totally unrelated to
each other, except on a surrealistic
level. For other examples of
Samaras' use of waste or found
materials, see page 161.

Study for *The Gates Number 9* by
Chryssa, 1968, Plexiglas, metal and
neon, 17½ x 19 x 13. Reproduced
courtesy The Aldrich Museum,
Ridgefield, Conn. Photo by
Richard DiLiberto.

Compared to Samaras' *Box L* on
the opposite page, Chryssa's study
gives the impression of great
organization. The viewer knows that
there is a functional plan to the
design because the box works—it
lights up.

Study: Falling Man, 3 box landscape by Ernest Trova, 1966, Plexiglas, plastic and enameled bronze, 8¾ x 41 x 28. Reproduced courtesy of Pace Gallery, New York. Photo by Ferdinand Boesch.

Ernest Trova's *Falling Man Series* of boxes and constructions reflects his involvement with mechanical phenomena and with the image of the contemporary human being. Some of the constructions and boxes are mechanized to provide action and movement.

Early in his career as a painter he was influenced by de Kooning, but by 1961 he was almost totally involved with construction. His falling-man image—an armless and faceless human replica—emerged from a single work in the exhibition Recent Constructions and Collages (Some Living) held in St. Louis that year.

This single figure, in varying positions and multiples, appears in all of Trova's current work under the reference *Study: Falling Man.* Trova's alien, mechanical man is an indictment of the dehumanized quality of contemporary life.

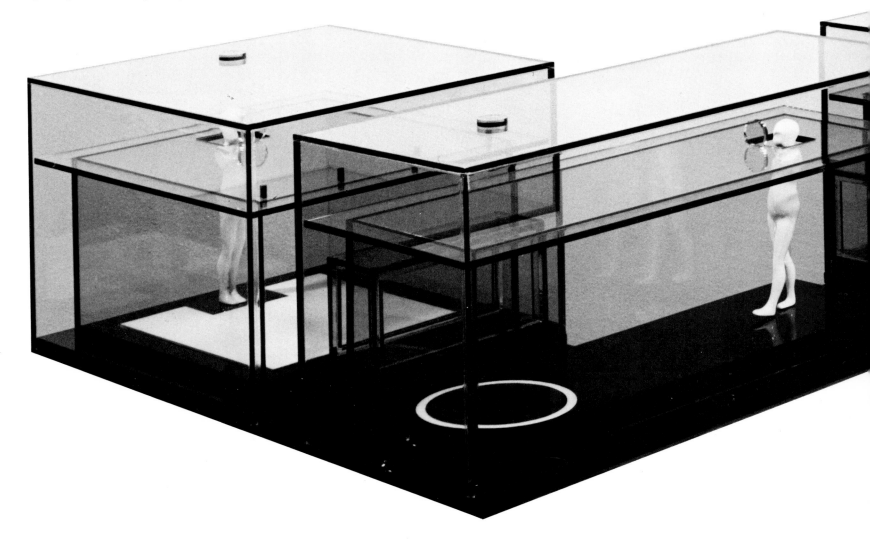

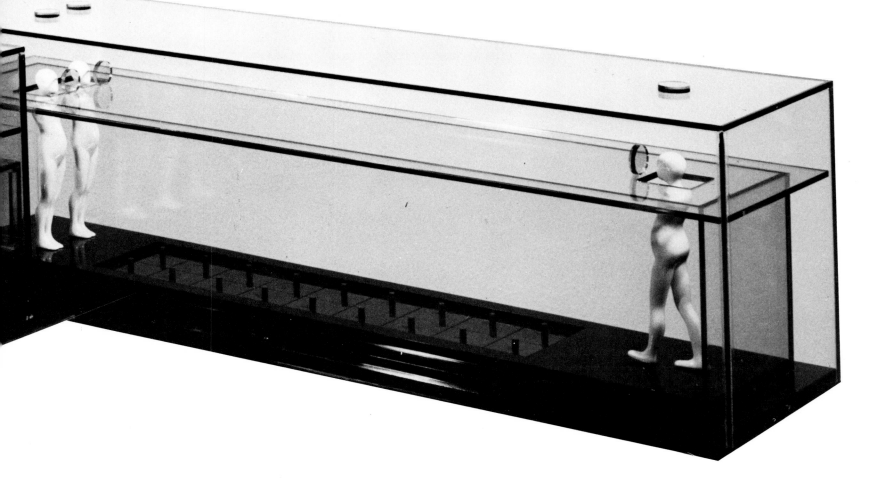

Mini-neon by Teruyuki Kunito. Displayed in the Vogue Interior Decorating Show. Reproduced courtesy Tokodo Shoten, Ltd., Tokyo.

An old-fashioned electric bulb contrasts with a futuristic filament of ascending numbers, a highly polished, curved stainless-steel base and a jet black environment to produce the excitement one expects from an "electrifying" box.

The Art Machine, No. 2 by Minoru Yoshida, 1968. Reproduced courtesy *Art in America*.

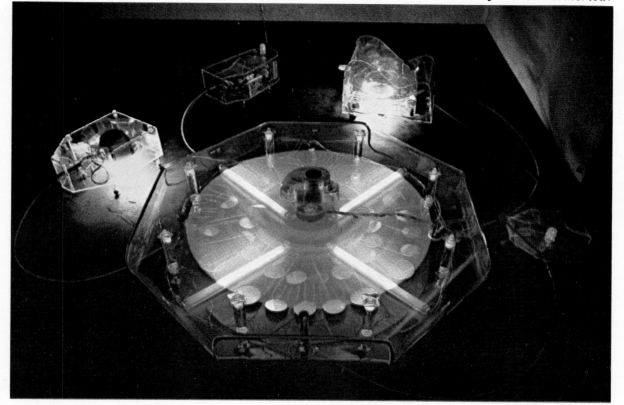

Electric Boxes

Electric power is one of the very most important energy resources of our time, and it seems only natural, therefore, for the artists of this era to employ it as a medium for artistic communication and expression. Within a single decade, "light art" or "electric art" has progressed from the simple use of a mechanical switch and a single light bulb to the integration of highly complex electronic circuitry and extremely sophisticated electronic components. Chryssa, reportedly, was inspired by, and found aesthetic expression in, the neon lights of New York City, while an artist like Stephen Antonakos, for instance, sees in neon the great potential for drawing in the blackness of space. The possibilities of electricity as a medium of artistic expression are endless.

It is only natural for the concept of the box or the container to be a vital part of this electric or light art form, for not only must the functional parts of the structures be housed, and at times shielded from the viewer, but the box can serve as a stage for the performance of the composition. And "performance" it is, for by its very nature electric light pulses with excitement and potential.

This chapter by no means represents all the artists working in light or electric art. Like the potential of these new media, work of merit in this area is developing and unfolding at a lightning pace, and any collection would be outdated as soon as it was made.

Blue Box by Stephen Antonakos,
1965/69, blue neon, 48 inches high.
Collection Naomi Spector.
Reproduced courtesy of the artist.

In his earlier compositions,
Antonakos, for the most part, used
cloth and found objects in order to
convert the familiar object to one
that was totally unfamiliar. In the
early 1960s Antonakos became
attracted to the potentialities of
neon tubing—both the color
possibilities and the pliability of
the material. With its great capability
for producing a condition of change
within a work, neon art represented
a challenge to him, and the resulting
sculpture and boxes are patterned
on formal arrangements of straight
and curved lines of color and light.

Opposite page

Electric boxes by Stephen Antonakos
*Above, left. Red Outside Corner Box
Neon,* 1972.

Above, right. Ruby and Yellow Neon,
1967, neon-tubing and enameled
white aluminum box with formica
base, 28½ x 36 x 36. Collection
Molly McGreevy. Reproduced
courtesy of the artist.

Below, left. The Room, 1973, neon
tubes, electrical equipment, 16 x
16 x 12 feet.

*Below, right. Blue Box Inside
Corner Box,* 1971.

In his *Ruby and Yellow Neon*
composition, the box holds the motor
that controls the sequence of the
lighting, while the layers of yellow,
white, pink and ruby neon tubing
crisscross the top like a series of
awnings or roofs. *The Room* was
exhibited at the Grand Rapids,
Michigan outdoor show, Sculpture
Off The Pedestal, in 1973. It is a
hollow lighted box with drawings
in neon at the top four corners
of the structure.

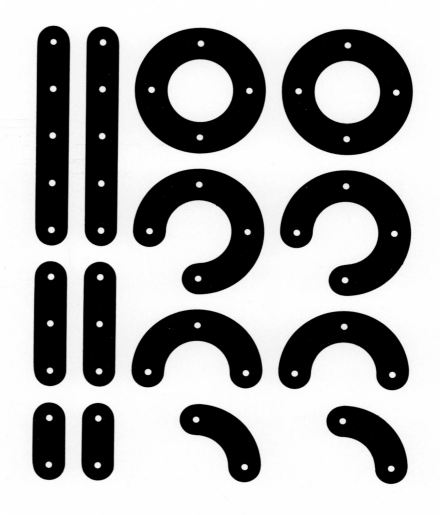

Above. A to X. Below. Unit for Numbers. Both boxes by Teruyuki Kunito were displayed in the Vogue Interior Decorating Show, 1970. Reproduced courtesy Tokodo Shoten Ltd., Tokyo.

Opposite page

Infinite Time by Teruyuki Kunito displayed in the Vogue Interior Decorating Show, 1970. Reproduced courtesy Tokodo Shoten Ltd., Tokyo.

Kunito attempts to ally the machine with the spirit of man. His clock box is transparent, as if suspended in space, and his numbers have a fleeting feeling about them for they seem to telescope progressively into each other like time itself. The box contains the clock's figures and mechanical works as though they were the stars in some distant galaxy.

Somehow, in looking at Kunito's collector's clock to find an exact point with respect to time, time itself becomes quite unimportant.

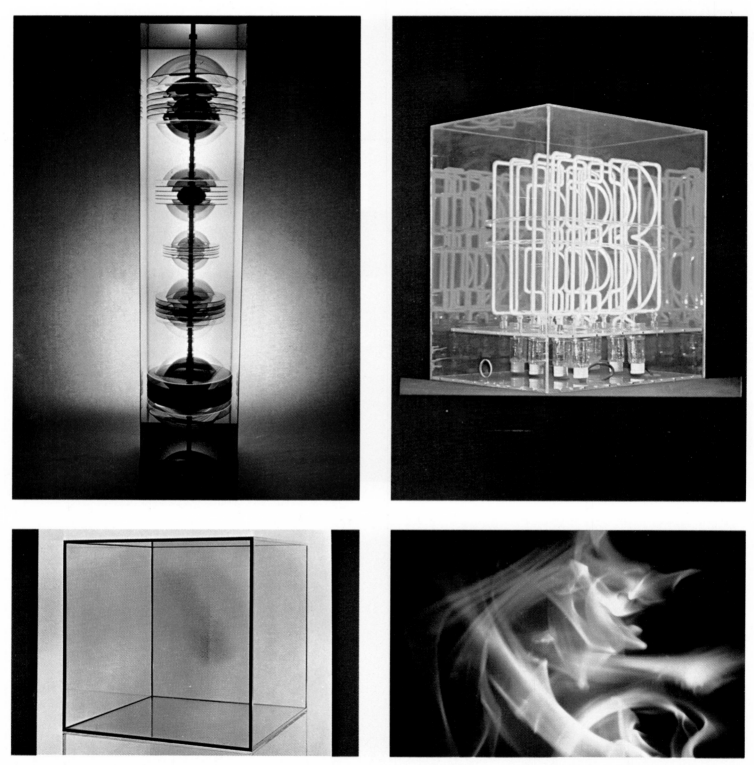

Top left. Spherical Plateau (front view) by Aaronel deRoy Gruber, 73½″ high (on 7 integral boxes) x 14¾ x 20¾. Five sections of circular rounded squares of predominantly blue and green acrylics. Reproduced courtesy of the artist.

Top right. Analysis of Letter B by Chryssa. Reproduced courtesy Art Education, Inc., New York.

Bottom left. Memories of Mike by Larry Bell, 1967, 24¼ x 24¼ x 24¼. Reproduced courtesy the artist. Collection Mr. and Mrs. Arnold B. Glimcher.

Each of the six sides of the cube is flat optical glass that has been coated on the inner surface by means of a vacuum-chamber process modified by the artist for his own use.

After Bell completed the coating process, the glass sheets were assembled, cemented at their beveled edges, and secured with strips of chrome-plated brass at the seams.

Bottom right. Lumia Light Sculpture by Earl Reiback, 1971. Reproduced courtesy of Galerie Moos Inc., Montreal.

How the sea can erode the hardest stone by Richard Prince, 1973, wood, plastic, glass, stone and electronic devices, 26 x 11 x 9. Reproduced courtesy of the artist.

Looking at the object from left to right: pressing the push button on the case causes current generated by the action of sea water on the zinc and copper plates (wet cell in the jar) to flow to a silicon control rectifier (small thing beside jar). This device electronically switches on a secondary circuit in which the batteries (12 volt lantern batteries) send current to a pulsing unit (little black box) which directs pulses of current to a solenoid coil (above large stone). This coil then repeatedly lifts up and drops a small pebble onto the large stone.

Lumia Light Sculpture by Earl Reiback, 1971. Reproduced courtesy of Galerie Moos, Inc., Montreal. Photo courtesy Waddell Gallery, New York.

Earl Reiback is a nuclear engineer whose kinetic "luminage" projections suggest the drifting of clouds and smoke through a brilliant choreography of orchestrated light and color. Presented in the form of a sizable box, the entire front of which is a screen, his luminous projections produce continuous, never-duplicated visual effects over a prolonged period of time, which defy classification and description.

Untitled by Chryssa, 1969, colored neon light encased in a Plexiglas box, 24 x 17 x 8. Reproduced courtesy of Multiples Inc., New York.

Silverman by Boyd Mefferd, 1967, aluminum, Plexiglas, and formica, two units, 42 x 36 x 16. Collection Walker Art Center, Minneapolis, gift of Northern States Power Company, Minneapolis. Photo by Eric Sutherland. Reproduced with kind permission.

Beginning with the study of realistic effects created by artificial lighting, Boyd Mefferd began experimentation with light itself through creating light boxes containing complex electronic components and equipment. His boxes, radiating colored lights that are manipulated by a complex electronic system of switching, create the effects of movement and of continuing motion that the viewer visualizes as a series of time intervals. In his notes, the artist has stated: "I believe that ultimately a purely time-dimensional approach to abstract composition is just as capable of communication as the abstract two- and three-dimensional work we have now . . ."

226

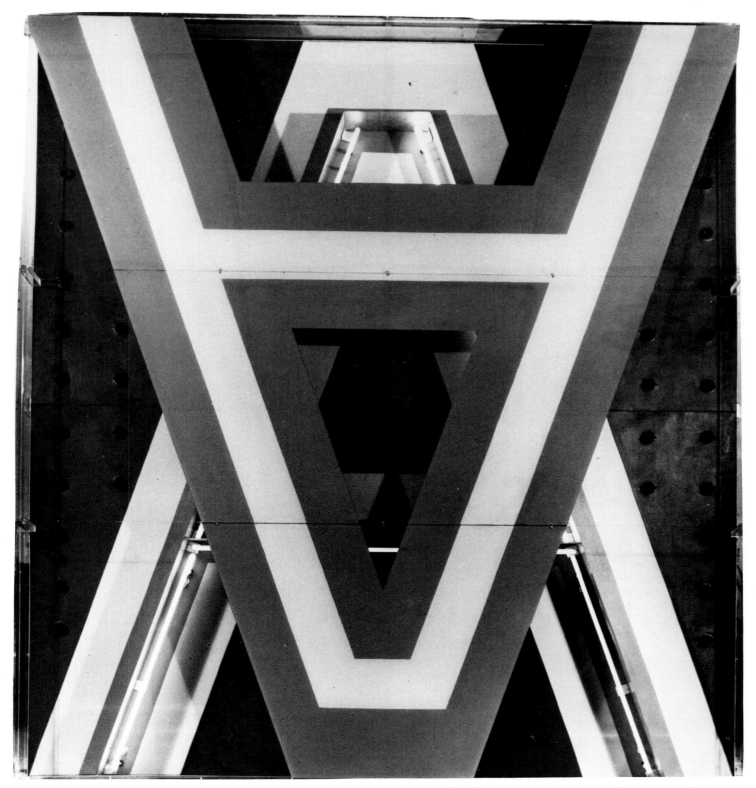

Construction A by Chryssa, 1970/73, oil on canvas, neon, Plexiglas and iron, 108 x 96 x 6. Reproduced courtesy Galerie Denise René, New York. Photo by Eric Pollitzer.

Chryssa's sculptures and boxes are in the form of neon, aluminum and Plexiglas, and her principal concentration is on calligraphic forms. Frequently Chryssa will take an individual letter from the alphabet and fragment it into lines and planes as if it were an analytical study (see *Analysis of Letter B,* page 224). Chryssa's compositions tend to create a total environment of architecture and sculpture, involving the viewer with the area that surrounds him. The flow and glow of the brightly colored neon illuminates both viewer and environment and melds the presence of one into the other.

Like others working with inventive and imaginative techniques and with contemporary materials, Chryssa's use of imagery is an aesthetic rendering of mass-production items and the mass-communication systems as we know them today.

Stainless Steel Hammer by Fletcher Benton. Reproduced courtesy of the artist. Photo by Roger Gass.

This composition, in the form of a highly polished T, has been set on its side and has blue and orange neon tubing inserted into its interior. The light is not functional, for it does not illuminate anything but its own presence, and is used purely for the aesthetic values it contributes to the work.

Synchronetic by Fletcher Benton, 1967, aluminum, Plexiglas, formica, fluorescent light, 16 x 49 x 4¾. Reproduced courtesy The Aldrich Museum, Ridgefield, Conn. Photo by Peter Moore.

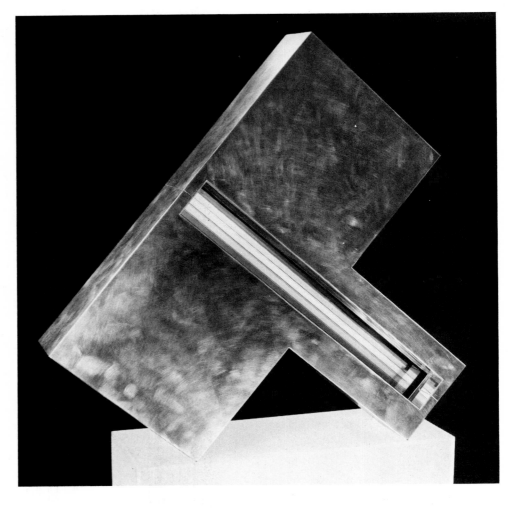

Compared to the *Stainless Steel Hammer,* in *Synchronetic* we have a large and glamorous setting for neon-tube lighting. The neon is no longer in an isolated position for meditation; instead, an entire composition using light structures to dictate a new art form has been created.

In a great many of his works, Benton uses moving, transparent Plexiglas panels of color, which overlap and/or slide past each other, and in this way produce constantly changing mixtures of color. His fusion of sophisticated stainless-steel pieces with color and motion represents a unique addition to the art of electric boxes.

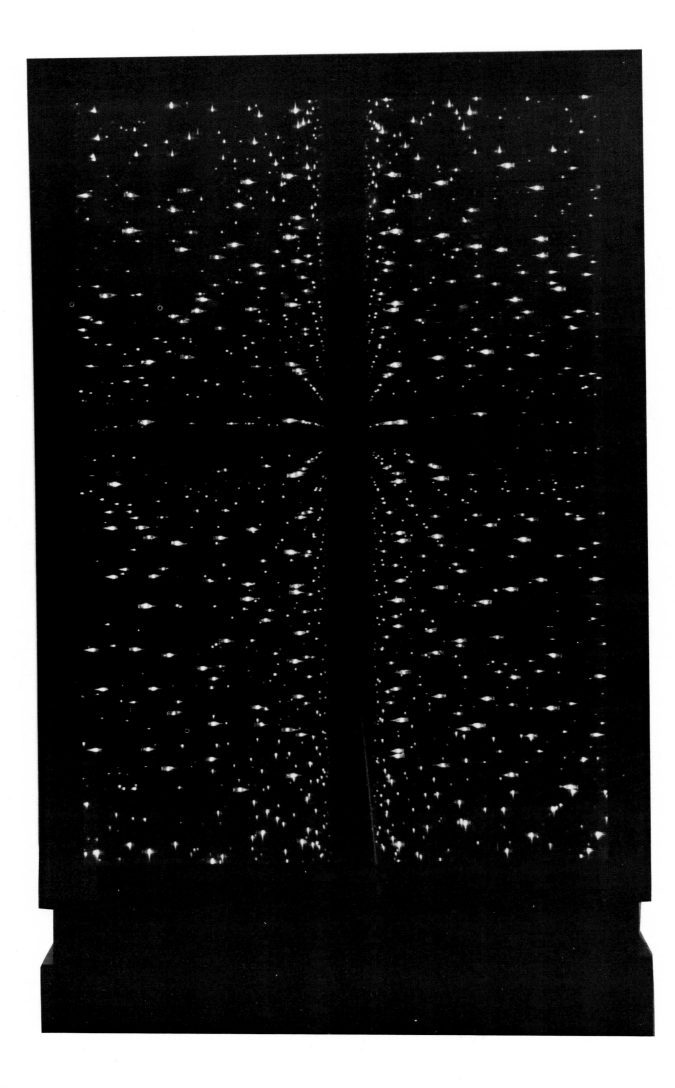

Luminaire by Aaronel deRoy Gruber, 66 x 31½ x 18. Lighted acrylic box with two-way glass front. Reproduced courtesy of the artist. Photo by Harry S. Coughanour.

Page 229

Cordova (detail) by Stanley Landsman, 1967, mixed media, 73¾ x 27½ x 33½. Collection Walker Art Center, Minneapolis, gift of Northern States Power Company, Minneapolis. Photo by Eric Sutherland. Reproduced with kind permission.

Page 230

Untitled by Stanley Landsman, 1967, glass, wood casing and electric lights, 71 x 27 x 24. Reproduced courtesy The Aldrich Museum, Ridgefield, Conn.

Beginning as an abstract expressionist, Landsman worked at reducing his color to minimal black and white, changing from canvas to Plexiglas and at times to glass mirror surfaces. Landsman began experimentation with mirrors and chromium-coated glass, for these provided potentialities creating compositions visually much larger than their basic physical dimensions. By containing a series of strategically arranged geometrically shaped mirrors and a number of light sources in the interior of his box construction, a fluctuating composition simulating the mystery and majesty of the heavens bursts upon and captivates the viewer.

Pages 232–235

Explosion by Tim Burns. Photograph courtesy Fine Art Workshop.

At the Liverpool, New South Wales, Australia Art Show, wooden boxes constructed by Tim Burns are wired by a high-frequency switch system and loaded with small quantities of gunpowder. The audience can activate the charge in each of the boxes by applauding, whistling, shouting or making the particular type of noise to which the implanted ignition has been made sensitive.

The Doty Boxes. Sixteen cardboard boxes identical in size, with a portion of a design printed on each individual box side, by Donald Doty. See also pages 3, 4, and 8.

By arranging the boxes in different sequence and order, the 96 sides are capable of combining to form an almost endless stream of designs and patterns.

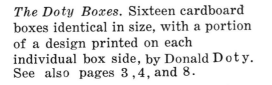

236

Index of Artists